Michael R. Reaves

LIFE TECHNIQUES IN GESTALT THERAPY

LIFE TECHNIQUES IN GESTALT THERAPY

—Edited by—
Joen Fagan and
Irma Lee Shepherd

PERENNIAL LIBRARY
Harper & Row, Publishers
New York, Evanston, San Francisco, London

To Fritz . . . a profound and disturbing teacher

This book originally appeared as Part Two of *Gestalt Therapy Now: Theory, Techniques, Applications,* which was published by Science and Behavior Books.

Three essays have been deleted from Part Two of the original book. They are: James S. Simkin, "Mary: A Session with a Passive Patient"; Henry T. Close, "Gross Exaggeration with a Schizophrenic Patient"; and Ruth C. Cohn, "A Child with a Stomachache: Fusion of Psychoanalytic Concepts and Gestalt Techniques."

LIFE TECHNIQUES IN GESTALT THERAPY
 For information address Harper & Row, Publishers, Inc., 10 East 53d Street, New York, N.Y. 10022. Published simultaneously in Canada by Fitzhenry & Whiteside Limited, Toronto.

First PERENNIAL LIBRARY edition published 1973.

STANDARD BOOK NUMBER: 06-080281-2

73 1

CONTENTS

Preface vii

Introduction 1

1 The Tasks of the Therapist 9
Joen Fagan

2 An Introduction to Gestalt Techniques 40
John B. Enright

3 One Gestalt Therapist's Approach 69
Laura Perls

4 Therapy in Groups: Psychoanalytic, Experiential, and Gestalt 77
Ruth C. Cohn

5 The Rules and Games of Gestalt Therapy 93
Abraham Levitsky and Frederick S. Perls

6 Experiential Psychotherapy with Families 108
Walter Kempler

7 Ann: Gestalt Techniques with a Woman with Expressive Difficulties 125
Joen Fagan

8 Dream Seminars 165
Frederick S. Perls

9 Limitations and Cautions in the Gestalt Approach 200
Irma Lee Shepherd

PREFACE

This collection grew from the awareness of the editors of the increased interest in Gestalt therapy among psychotherapists throughout the country. The most extensive influence has been the lectures and demonstrations by Dr. Frederick Perls, Dr. Laura Perls, Dr. James Simkin, and others, presented before national and regional meetings of psychiatrists, psychologists, and psychotherapists. Further intensive involvement came from Gestalt workshops and training institutes held regularly at Esalemn Institute at Big Sur, California; at the Gestalt Therapy Institutes in Los Angeles, New York, and Cleveland; and workshops in other cities. About a thousand therapists participated in these workshops, and more than two hundred therapists across the country identify themselves as being Gestalt or Gestalt-oriented.[1] The *Directory* of the American Academy of Psychotherapists lists Gestalt therapy as the sixth most common affiliation, with more members than better known or more extensively published schools such as Jungian or Rational-Emotive. Despite the increasing involvement of psychotherapists who find the concepts and techniques of Gestalt therapy exciting, intriguing, and effective, little written material is available, the major exceptions being Dr. Perls's two early and still basic books, *Ego,*

[1] *Directory of Gestalt Therapists.* Beverly Hills, Calif.: Robbert Resnick, 1969.

Hunger and Aggression (1949, 1969) and *Gestalt Therapy* (1951).

There are several reasons for the scarcity of published material on Gestalt therapy. Dr. Perls, who, with the assistance of his wife Laura, is responsible for the beginning and early development of Gestalt therapy, initially worked in relative professional isolation in South Africa and has shown little interest in creating a "school" of therapy as such. Also, Gestalt therapy, with its emphasis on the here and now, the immediacy of experience, and nonverbal expressiveness, and its avoidance of "aboutisms" or overuse of the mental "computer," tends to correct our tendencies toward wordiness and abstractions rather than to encourage the manipulation of words necessary for the writing of books. Thus, most Gestalt therapists tend to be doers rather than sayers.

Finally, in Gestalt therapy, much importance is attached to tone of voice, posture, gestures, facial expression, etc., with much of the import and excitement coming from work with changes in these nonverbal communications. Transcribing these into type is difficult and loses much of the meaning and immediacy. Fortunately the increasing availability of Gestalt films and tapes helps in making the nonverbal communications more accessible.

In spite of the above problems, the need for available material on Gestalt therapy is marked. The present collection attempts to bring Dr. Perls's work into historical focus and to present his most recent thinking. A wide (though not exhaustive) sampling of techniques and applications from a number of therapists and teachers is offered.

The book is intended for the Gestalt therapist; for

the psychotherapist of some other orientation who wishes to explore new ideas that may be stimulating and applicable in his own practice; for the therapist-in-training who wishes to become acquainted with recent developments in therapy; and for the sophisticated layman who is interested in ways of feeling, relating, and behaving other than those offered by our work-ridden, past-oriented, computer-programmed and game-laden modern life. This book will, of course, not give any complete or final answers, nor is it any replacement for actual training in or experience with Gestalt techniques. However, it should serve at least to point toward some of the exciting developments occurring in psychotherapy, and to suggest the increased capacity for living that they offer.

INTRODUCTION

Techniques or therapeutic procedures are central to any therapy endeavor. Techniques arise from two sources, coming in part from the theoretical underpinnings of a specific "school" or approach and in part from the therapist's ongoing treatment interactions, where the requirement of "making something happen" exists. Out of his boredom, frustration, desperation, inspiration, and/or creativity, a therapist will periodically devise new procedures or approaches. When these work, he will extend them to other patients and begin developing a rationale or theory. Techniques therefore both feed into and out from theory. If the techniques can be taught and are useful to other therapists, then a specific approach develops. Both the techniques that a therapist devises and those that he adopts from others must have some degree of congruity with his own personality make-up before he can use them effectively. The therapist who is able to use Gestalt techniques effectively generally prefers activity to passivity, accepts power but does not need it for personal gratification, acts with firmness and assurance, enjoys improvising rather than following a fixed plan, is not unduly afraid of intense emotional explosions, and can utilize himself and his emotional reactions without great fear of exposure. Persons who have high investments in cognitive or "computer" processes, who prefer emotional distance, who tend to be conservative, who prefer to reflect or "follow" the patient's responses, or who lack awareness of their own experience have more difficulty with Gestalt techniques.

Gestalt techniques offer considerable flexibility in their usefulness. Perhaps their greatest contribution lies in their utilization in day, weekend, or month workshops where their variety, power, and immediacy quickly involve participants, foster rapid "knowing" of others, and produce vivid personality change. The techniques are also of considerable value for long-term individual therapy, and may be utilized, with appropriate caution, for a wide variety of people and problems. (For instance, the papers that follow describe therapy with children and adults, normal, neurotic, and psychotic, seen individually, in groups, or with the family.) Gestalt techniques can be used in productive combination with a variety of other approaches. Finally, they are adaptable to use with one's self and, if necessary, colleagues. However, they need to be approached with caution and full respect for their ability to have powerful effects. It is not intended nor expected that reading these papers can make even an experienced therapist into a "Gestaltist" without personal experience and training. Nor are the papers intended in any way as a "cookbook" for the inexperienced.

A number of problems have traditionally been associated with the general topic of techniques. Five of these will be explored briefly, with references to the papers that deal with some of the issues at more length. In general, the directness and immediacy of theory and practice in Gestalt therapy have contributed to the reduction of many dichotomies that have been persistent problems for psychotherapists.

Inconsistencies between theory and techniques. Beginning with Freud, many theories of therapy have seemed only remotely connected to the specific operations of the therapist. For example, if psychoanalysis views the core of maladjustment to be instinctual and sexual, with problems produced in part by man's basic nature and in part by impulses blocked and distorted by past experiences, then it does not follow directly that adjustment should come as a result of communicating verbally, in a situation with many limitations, to a relatively unresponsive therapist. Similarly, while Fromm was writing his most important books detailing the sources of men's problems as residing in the economic and political structure of society, he was attempting to treat these ills by individual therapy. However, in Gestalt therapy the theory that people's problems arise from their lack of awareness and from the ways in which they block awareness leads directly to the therapist's focusing attention on this area and offering suggestions, tasks, and exercises designed either to promote awareness in general or to assist an individual with his specific avoidances. Also, the patient's stated problems or concerns are translated directly into the therapy situation and in essence are demonstrated rather than simply described.

Discrepancy between artificial techniques and genuine response. This issue is discussed in several of the articles that follow, especially those by Fagan, Cohn, and Kempler. Briefly, the Gestalt therapist follows the same directions that he gives to the patient, staying with his own awareness. His awareness will most often, without real effort on his part, be focused on the patient and his words, movements, tone of voice, etc. As he becomes aware of discrepancies, he will almost automatically translate these into suggestions and experiments for the patient. If the patient refuses or resists, or if the therapist responds with boredom, irritation, or perplexity, then his attention will switch from the patient to himself, and his own experiences will hold center stage in his awareness. He must then find ways of resolving these, by withdrawing, verbalizing them, etc., which is usually part of the same process as helping the patient to the next step in awareness. If the therapist continues to feel blocked, then he will utilize the same procedures for himself that he might suggest to a patient. If, during the process of therapy, a memory, joke, personal experience, or idea emerges strongly, then the therapist will probably choose to share it in a routine way. In short, the Gestalt therapist believes that he can be only what he is in the situation and that the procedures he suggests for the patient are the ones he follows himself. He experiences little dichotomy and views the problem of techniques versus authenticity, which has been subject to many heated debates in other therapeutic approaches, as practically a dead issue.

Emphasis on historical material versus present happenings. The Gestalt emphasis on the *now* often leads to important and affect-laden memories. When this occurs, the past is made present by the use of the present tense and the enactment of interactions. It is generally taboo in Gestalt procedures to allow past history to be simply talked about.

Status difference and distance between therapist and patient. The Gestalt therapist is, and regards himself as, an expert. This does not imply, however, that he regards the patient as inferior or different. He realizes the potential interchangeability of patient and therapist roles, and indeed has found himself on many occasions wrestling with his own blocks and unfinished business. He is also more than willing to leave the patient and therapist roles in the therapy situation and, once outside, respond and interact on a personal and social basis, avoiding as necessary, however, contact with the person who cannot leave behind the patient position. In groups an artificial distinction may sometimes be enforced by the therapist, who usually has specific directions or procedures in mind in working with a patient; if a group member insists on "breaking in" and being helpful, he may be put down gently or asked to explore his own projections.

Discrepancy between the therapeutic situation and "real life." While the structure and limits of therapy do make distinctions between it and other aspects of living, the experiencing is not artificial nor remote.

Of the papers that follow, "The Tasks of the Therapist" (Fagan) attempts to spell out the skills and characteristics needed by the therapist, dividing them into five categories: patterning, control, potency, humanness, and commitment. Fagan describes the contributions to and difficulties with each of these in a number of therapeutic approaches, as well as some of the contributions of Gestalt therapy.

"Techniques of Gestalt Therapy" (Enright) describes goals and strategy, tactics and techniques. Enright begins by defining attention and awareness, and suggests that an appropriate way to conceptualize maladjustment is to view it as blocks in the development of awareness. Therapy basically consists of the reintegration of attending and awareness, with the emphasis placed on helping the patient develop his own problem-solving capacity rather than letting the therapist attempt to solve his problems for him. The therapist's awareness of the patient's blocks and incongruencies results in techniques to bring these obstacles to the patient's attention in various ways. Enright gives a number of excellent examples and procedural strategies. There are four main ways in which patients block awareness: retroflection, when the person opposes and holds back wishes, impulses, and behaviors, resulting in unfinished business; desensitization of sensory and physical messages; introjection of other's "shoulds"; and projection of expectations, criticisms, etc., onto other persons. Finally, Enright discusses six issues from the Gestalt point of view: the actual therapeutic agent or change-producer; who decides when to terminate; the range of applicability; work with dreams; the use of the therapist as a person; and utilization of the past. Turning specifically to Gestalt procedures, Laura Perls answers questions dealing with her approach to some of the typical problems presented by patients, including motivation, physical contact, and the personal involvement of the therapist. "Psychoanalytic, Experiential, and Gestalt Therapy in Groups" (Cohn) utilizes wide experience with group therapy in a comparative study of the theory, goals, procedures, and techniques of the three approaches. Cohn includes her own subjective reactions and her observations of student responses to Gestalt workshops and demonstrations.

"Rules and Games of Gestalt Therapy" (Levitsky and Perls) supplies a compendium of suggestions for increasing direct confrontation and awareness, and in assisting the patient to assume responsibility. These "rules" are applied generally, but not dogmatically, in Gestalt sessions, with the patient being reminded or corrected when he has broken their letter or spirit. Then a number of Gestalt games are described. These have several purposes, including warming up a group, involving the entire group, and assisting specific individuals.

"Experiential Psychotherapy with Families" (Kempler) describes the utilization of Gestalt techniques by a therapist who integrates them with his personal and emotional responses in a direct and immediate way. Kempler gives a rationale for his approach and several examples of his interaction with families.

"Gestalt Techniques with a Woman with Expressive Difficulties" (Fagan) reports on a set of exercises and experiments designed to assist a student who had major blocks in written and oral communication. The "Diary of a Girl with Blue Paint on Her Nose," which follows, contains the student's account of her experiences. While there are many accounts by therapists of their procedures and a number of first-hand reports by patients (usually written in retrospect rather than during the process), there are few that have reported the same experience from both sides as it was occurring.

"Two Dream Seminars" (Perls) presents a brief description of Perls's ideas concerning the importance and use of dreams and then demonstrates his approach with four volunteers. The first dreamer, as she plays through some of the objects, persons, and animals in her dream, begins to come to grips with her conflict between power and passivity, or between masculine and feminine aspects of herself, and works toward a partial resolution. The second dream deals with a conflict between sterile artificiality and deeply buried creativity. The third dream opens up an important piece of unfinished business, with the dreamer becoming intensely involved in the struggle between being independent and being cared for by her mother at the cost of helplessness and lack of self-support. The rapid progression of emotional responses from helplessness, to the expression of anger toward her mother, to sadness at giving up the old pattern is a very typical one. The fourth dream vividly illustrates a patient's attempts to impress others by taking risks, and the importance to him of gaining others' liking and acceptance at the cost of suppressing his fear and anger. He is encouraged to face his catastrophic expectations of death and/or rejection. Utilizing members of the group as projection screens is illustrated. It is interesting to note that while the first and second dreams share several types of content and include similar behaviors, as do the third and fourth, working out the dreams results in very different meanings to the dreamers.

Finally, Shepherd discusses "Limitations and Cautions in the Gestalt Approach." She describes a number of areas where the therapist using Gestalt techniques needs to be aware of possible difficulties or dangers and suggests ways of avoiding unfortunate outcomes in these areas.

chapter 1

THE TASKS OF THE THERAPIST

Joen Fagan

All professional persons are basically problem solvers who are employed to reduce discomfort or conflict and to increase the possibilities of certain valued outcomes for the persons who request their assistance.* Therapists, specifically, are engaged by persons who are dissatisfied with their own, or another's experiencing and behaving, which may include internal experiences of anxiety, discomfort, conflict, or dissatisfaction, and external behaviors that are either inadequate or insufficient for the tasks at hand or that result in difficulties with other people. The problems presented to the therapist may be central to the person and require extensive changes, or they may be peripheral and quickly solved. Not only the problems are varied, but also therapists differ widely, both in their procedures and in their effectiveness with different kinds of persons and problems. I believe that therapists and therapeutic techniques will become increasingly specialized and increasingly effective, partially as a function of

* While this article deals specifically with therapists, the tasks described can be modified and extrapolated to describe any professional group.

research and partially as a function of rapidly growing willingness to experiment with a variety of new techniques. However, while many changes will occur, the basic tasks of the therapist will remain similar. The purpose of this chapter is to examine the tasks or requirements of the therapeutic endeavor under five headings: patterning, control, potency, humanness, and commitment; to indicate briefly the contributions of various approaches or "schools" to each of these; and to focus on contributions from Gestalt therapy.

Patterning

The therapist is first of all a perceiver and constructor of patterns. As soon as he is informed of a symptom or a request for change, and begins listening to and observing a patient and responding to him, he begins a process that I refer to as *patterning*. While *diagnosis* is a more common term, it has the disadvantage of provoking the analogy of the medical model and implying that the purpose of the process is arriving at a specific label. A better analogy for the process of patterning is that of artistic creation, involving sometimes cognitive, sometimes perceptual and intuitive skills in interaction with the material and demands of the environment as, for example, in the creation of a mobile, in which a variety of pieces or systems are interconnected into an overall unity and balance.

As the therapist begins his contact with the patient requesting help, he has available a body of theory which is largely cognitive in nature, a background of past experience, and a number of awarenesses and personal responses derived from the ongoing interaction that have large emotional and intuitive components. From these, which may be given varying degrees of importance by a specific therapist, he begins to form an understanding of the interaction of events and systems that result in a given life style that supports a given symptom pattern. *Events* refers to the things that have happened or do happen to the patient; *systems* includes all those interlocking events that interact on a specific level of existence, such as biological systems, self-perception systems, family systems, etc. The patient is visualized as a focal point of many systems, including the cellular, historical, economic, etc. The more the therapist can specify the entire interaction, or be sensitive to the possible effects of systems he is not directly concerned with (such as the neurological), or intuit the connecting points between systems where the most strain exists, the more effective he can be in producing change. He can act on a level and at a point that promises the most positive change in symptoms or conflicts at the least cost of effort, and where the least disruptive change will occur to other systems.

An example may clarify some of the above description. A mother refers her son whose increasing stomach distress causes him frequently to stay home from school. The therapist shortly begins to accumulate information of various sorts. He learns that: the boy also has stomachaches that keep him from going to camp or from visiting relatives; the mother has few interests outside the home; the father does not like his job and also has frequent illnesses; the mother and father have intercourse very infrequently; the boy has average intelligence; the grandmother is very interested in his becoming a doctor; the other children tease him for being a sissy; his teacher is considered strict; the school system has a new superintendent who has made many changes, etc. The therapist observes that the boy waits for his mother to answer for him; that his voice is weak when he does answer; and so on through a long list of responses, observations, and experiments in which the therapist obtains some sort of assessment of the abilities of the boy and his family to respond to varying suggestions and pressures. Through these processes a picture emerges with increasing clarity. The boy, his stomach, his family, his peer group, the school, the school system, and the community come into focus with varying degrees of explicitness.

We first label our understanding of the crux of the problem and then move to intervene on one or possibly several levels, depending on our personal preference, style, and understanding. No matter how badly we do initially in spotting the interactions that are most important, there is a clear possibility that intervention on any level may sooner or later produce the changes we wish, since the systems are interlocking and a change in one system may produce changes in some or many of the other systems. (This may be paraphrased, "Everyone has a little bit of the truth.") We may start with a medical approach, choosing antispasmodics, antiemetics, or tranquilizers. We may attempt to produce primarily internal psychological changes by play therapy, hypnosis, rational-emotive procedures, or desensitization. We may attempt to set up environmental learning situations by academic coaching or by activity group therapy. We may use behavior modification by observing the ways in which the mother reinforces the boy's avoidance behavior and may work with her to change these. We may see the mother individually to help her change her perception of mothering, support her in developing outside interests, or involve her in sensitivity training. We may work with the father in exploring his frequent illnesses or in helping him to find more job satisfaction. We may select couple therapy to assist the parents in dealing with their sexual problems and developing a more satisfactory marriage. We may use family therapy to increase communication, clarify the parents' interactions with the boy, and find ways of modifying the grandmother's influence. It is also possible to arrange environmental changes, such as changing teachers or schools. We could work with the teacher or school counselor, and finally (but grandiosely) we could envision involving the school system, the community, or eventually, the country.

No matter what procedures are chosen, we will need to evaluate our results by three main criteria: how rapidly the symptom has been removed, what positive behavior has replaced it, and how little disturbance has been created in the interlocking systems. These areas of evaluation will be discussed at more length in the section on techniques that follows.

Each therapy system has its own rationale and its own ideas about personality and procedure. Techniques are designed to intervene at the place or places where the theory says the pattern can most easily be modified. All theories and techniques fail at times because no two patterns are exactly alike and the points of conflict may vary widely. However, all theories that are taken seriously have some successes since changes in any system can affect others.

The Gestalt contribution to patterning involves a de-emphasis on cognitive theory and provides extensive assistance with the therapist's own awareness. Enright, in Chapter 2, describes this process in detail, emphasizing the clues to underlying events and life styles that can be uncovered by awareness of the person's movements, tones, expressions, word choice, etc., and suggesting some appropriate techniques for exploration. Much of Gestalt patterning is worked out in the therapy process itself rather than by history-taking or interviewing. The meanings that result, as in dream work, are very different from the more traditional analytic interpretive approaches where certain meanings are specified in advance by theory or predicted from the patient's previous history. Of course, past events of much importance do arise from the process of exploring posture, gestures, and dreams. However, the Gestalt therapist is not interested in the historical reconstruction of the patient's life, nor in weighing the effects of various environmental forces, nor in focusing upon one specific behavior such as communication style. Rather, he is interested in a global way in the point of contact between the various systems available for observation. The interactions between a person and his body, between his words and his tone of voice, between his posture and the person he is talking to, between himself and the group he is a member of are the focal points. The Gestalt therapist does not hypothesize nor make inferences about other systems that he cannot observe, though he may ask the patient to reenact *his* perceptions of them, as in a dialogue with his father, for example. Most Gestalt procedures are designed to bear upon the point of intersection, and the nature of the other system is viewed as less important than how the patient perceives or reacts to it.

In other words, the patterning emphasis in Gestalt therapy is on the process of interaction itself, including the patient's skills in fostering and risking interaction, or blocking awareness and change. Since these are skills of importance in the intersection of any systems from the biological through the social, the Gestalt therapist sees himself as preparing the individual to interact more effectively in all aspects of life. Perls's ideas concerning a therapeutic community, which he is presently formulating, represent a possible extension of Gestalt thinking to a more extensive system.

CONTROL

No matter how clear and adequate the therapist's patterning is, he must be able immediately to exercise control or nothing else can follow. Control is defined as the therapist's being able to persuade or coerce the patient into following the procedures he has set, which may include a variety of conditions. Control is not used here with cynicism or a Svengali attitude, nor is there any implication of ignoring the value of genuine concern and liking for the patient; it simply reflects the reality that unless patients do some of the things that therapists suggest, little will happen, and that which does happen will be mostly by accident.

Whitaker (1968) makes this idea very explicit: "Therapy has to begin with a fight . . . a fight over who controls the context of therapy. . . . I want it understood that I'm in charge of what happens. I see this as the administrative battle I have to win [in Haley and Hoffman, 1968, pp. 266, 267]" (a number of other therapists have written extensively about the importance of control: Haley, 1961 a, 1961 b, 1963; Rosen, 1953.)

Haley and Erickson often use a paradoxical double-bind, a command so phrased that there is no way of disobeying it, or disobedience involves making admissions that are extremely damaging or revealing. These not only maintain control but often contribute to a very rapid reduction in symptoms. Rosen, Bach, and others often use group pressure as a means of control. A patient may be able to meet or defeat the therapist in a fight, but his chances against eight or ten people who are aware of what he is attempting are very slim.

Part of the importance of control is that all symptoms represent indirect ways of trying to control or force others into certain patterns of behavior. The therapist has to counter being controlled by the patient's symptom pattern and also establish the conditions he needs to work. Some of the conditions will be overt behavioral requirements, such as keeping appointments, paying, bringing other family members, etc. Other conditions will be more overt or implicit, such as the willingness to give information, attempt suggestions, or produce fantasies. While the required aspects of external behavior vary from therapist to therapist, it is essential that the conditions most important to him be met to his reasonable satisfaction. It is common knowledge that patients who initially ask for special favors or conditions, such as special appointment times or reduced fees, will be more difficult to work with; and the therapist often counters by setting up stronger-than-usual controls, such as payment at each interview or the use of a consultant.

Two of the major aspects of implicit control can be examined under the concepts of motivation and rapport. Motivation is often thought of as being related to the patient's discomfort or anxiety; the higher these are, the more the patient is willing to work. However, the degree of distress can be thought of with equal validity as the willingness of the patient to relinquish control to the therapist. Some persons who are experiencing marked distress are difficult to work with because they attribute their discomfort to others via blame. Their motivation for change is high but their willingness to surrender control is low.

Rapport is usually presented somewhat ideally as the "good feeling" and amount of positive relationship between patient and therapist; more accurately it is the therapist's ability to persuade the patient, or the patient's willingness to trust the therapist's control of the situation. While liking for the therapist is probably necessary somewhere along the therapeutic process, and of value even initially, it is probably more important in the early stages for the patient to believe that the therapist knows what he's doing.

The techniques the therapist uses to gain and maintain control are often, though not necessarily, different from the ones he uses to produce personality or behavioral change. (All techniques, of course, depend heavily on the style of the individual.) The therapist must recognize, manifest, and counter the patient's efforts at taking control by his usual means, some of which will be represented by his symptoms, others more deviously. He must manage to avoid being put off, frightened, or bored by the psychotic; to keep from being had by the psychopath or enjoying him too much; and to avoid being too sympathetic or agreeing with the neurotic's formulations. He must be able to remain his own man while also becoming enough involved with the patient's life style to experience its problems and difficulties.

A special problem is presented by the patient who comes because of external coercion, such as court order, divorce threat, or parent's commands. The situation is such that the external agent has the control, and the therapist runs the risk of becoming his hireling, ostensibly agreeing that he and the patient will work hard to please this outside person. The therapist has, however, at least three main ploys to regain control: he can involve the referring agent, thus indicating that both the agent and the patient need help; he can disavow the external payoff ("It's no concern of mine whether you flunk out of school"); or he can go along by an initial identification with the person's goals to contrast with the agent's as, for example, in Schwartz's (1967) and Greenwald's (1967) offering to make their patients into better psychopaths.

External compliance with a threatened punishment has an internal parallel—the pseudocompliance and "improvement" labeled by analysts as "intellectual insight" or "transference cure" and by transactional analysts as playing "Greenhouse" or "Psychiatry" or "Gee, You're a Wonderful Therapist" (Berne, 1964). Perls's label is "bear-trapper," which describes the patient who, having learned something about the expectations of the therapist, goes through the motions of cooperation, then at a crucial moment refuses to comply with suggestions, thus catching the therapist off balance. Often the bear-trapper is a person with considerable underlying pathology who has much invested in demonstrating that he cannot be helped or changed, and that those who try do not have the power to force him. In this situation, regaining control is difficult since the patient has made it clear that efforts on the part of the therapist to control only indicate an admission of his failure. Renouncing control and admitting failure is one way of regaining it.

Another problem of control can be anticipated with the patient whose presenting symptoms include psychosis or potential psychosis, suicide, and the more severe varieties of "acting out." These are persons who in the past have effectively utilized the threat, "If you don't do what I want, then I'll . . . (kill myself, go crazy, embarrass you, etc.)." These are potent threats and can invoke fear and self-doubts, or may even blackmail the therapist into acting in ways that jeopardize his purpose and position. Suicide or homicide are the ultimate threats, and each of these may force the therapist into assuming more control than he wishes—which, of course, admits that the patient is in control. One of the most effective ways of neutralizing such threats is to make a clear contract initially. Szasz (1965a) informs patients that they will need to make arrangements with someone else if they require hospitalization; Goulding (1967) requires signed contracts from potentially suicidal patients in which they agree without reservation to make no suicide attempts while they are seeing him.

Another type of control only now beginning to be explored systematically is that offered by total environments, such as prisons and mental hospitals. For many years we attempted to deny that external control, other than gross loss of liberty and bare conformity with institution procedures, was either important or desirable. The success of behavior-modification procedures, which make many of the bare amenities of living dependent on certain patient behaviors, is forcing a reevaluation of the position that external control is not appropriate for persons who are unwilling or unable to utilize internal control. The painfully sincere and extensive study by Rogers and his associates (1967) in which competent and dedicated men attempted to modify the behavior of chronic schizophrenics by ignoring external control and attempting to assist the recovery of internal control by nondirective therapy resulted in almost complete futility. It is becoming increasingly evident that in patterning and control, chronic schizophrenics have obliterated almost all of the usual systems and procedures, and can be approached initially most effectively by very specific controls related to the immediate environment. Evidence is also accumulating to suggest that treatment of acute schizophrenic episodes may be approached most effectively by treatment of the total family (Langsley et al., 1968). The major implication of environmental control as represented by behavior modification is that it is needed to the extent to which the individual is unable or unwilling to assume internal control; to the extent to which internal control is possible, external control is insulting, inefficient, or a violation of civil liberties.

Control is most important in the beginning of therapy. The need for control decreases as cooperative control by patient and therapist increases because of greater ability to communicate in each other's language and the development of trust. However, at important points of change, the struggle for control will reemerge, usually on a more intense level, and the therapist should be prepared to fight this battle periodically.

Even initially, the attempt to maintain complete control is impossible and the appearance needs to be periodically renounced, first as a paradoxical way of maintaining control and secondly as a way of encouraging the patient's own assumption of responsibility and growth. (An excellent example of this is found in Simkin's chapter "Mary," page 162.) However, the abandoning of control should be viewed as an occasional technique and not as a complete system, as in the early days of nondirective therapy, or in group situations (see, for example, Bion, 1961) where the leader refuses to assume a leadership role. The inevitable outcome is that the group, in order to fill the vacuum, engages in a struggle for leadership accompanied by considerable expression of anger. Since this is a systems effect, the leader cannot claim credit for having produced any special results, and the value to the participants is dubious. While the person whose electric supply is disrupted may be able to get along with candles and a fireplace, this demonstration of self-sufficiency is not what he is paying the power company to produce.

The Gestalt contribution to problems of control includes a number of responses and procedures. Initially the therapist encourages patient autonomy and minimizes struggles by telling the patient that if he has strong objections to complying with suggestions he can (has the therapist's permission to) refuse, and his refusal will be honored. However, he is told that he has to state his reason for refusal. Often, as the reason is given, it can be explored for validity ("What's so terrible about being embarrassed?") and the patient will decide to continue.

Gestalt therapists ask for a clear statement from the patient concerning what he wishes to accomplish. Proceeding from this central theme keeps the emphasis on the patient's stated wishes, not the therapist's expectations. Procedures that keep in the present and make it clear that the therapist is in sensitive awareness with what is happening also decrease resistance. (When a patient begins meeting opposition from his conflicts and the discomfort that surrounds them, he may clearly resist, but this is on a very different order from resistance of control.) The patient is often asked if he would be willing to try an experiment: an acceptance carries a mild commitment to continue, while a refusal is honored if a reason is given. The patient who freezes, draws a blank, or has nothing come to mind can be asked to verbalize his refusal more specifically or to take responsibility for it by saying, "I am making my mind blank." Another procedure is to go with the resistance ("Tell me that it's no business of mine what you're thinking") and then have the fantasied therapist answer back. The value of resistance can also be approached ("What are all the good reasons for refusing me now; what does refusing do for you that is valuable for you?").

POTENCY

To justify his hire, the therapist must be able to assist the patient to move in the direction that he wishes, that is, to accelerate and provoke change in a positive direction. We are rapidly leaving the time when the therapist, in the absence of more specific knowledge, relies on "something" in the relationship that will result in "something" happening. We are approaching the time when the therapist can specify procedures that promote rapid change in a way that the patient can experience directly and others can observe clearly. For a given patient, many of the changes that do occur are a direct or by-product of the therapeutic relationships as described in the next section on humanness. (The therapeutic relationship is both a technique and a transcendence of techniques.) However, the therapist has need at many points of techniques, procedures, experiments, gimmicks, directions, and suggestions that can overcome inertia and promote movement. The patient who asks for specific assistance should expect to receive it.

Techniques are one of the more publicized aspects of psychotherapy; everyone knows that Freudians interpret and analyze dreams, and others hypnotize, analyze transactions, give tokens, etc. With increasing speed and accuracy, we are able to remove symptoms and change behaviors such as phobias, sexual deviations, inhibitions, etc., that only a few years ago were thought to require extended treatment. The increasing power of the therapist has resurrected two old topics that have a long history: the question of therapist authenticity versus techniques and the problem of symptom substitution.

The existentialists and neo-Rogerians (Rogers, 1951; Bugental, 1965; Carkhuff and Berenson, 1967) write powerfully of the human condition and the need for genuine relationships. However, techniques are often ignored or decried as being artificial, with the implication that authenticity cannot occur in their presence. I observed one of the most highly respected existential therapists in the country leading a group that was being observed by several hundred people and video-taped as a record of his way of working. The group, composed of student volunteers, spent over forty minutes continuing to be uncomfortably aware of the audience and verbalizing their discomfort at being observed and expected to produce. The therapist periodically shared with the group his own anxiety, self-consciousness, and fears that nothing would happen. When, at the end of the hour, a group member finally volunteered a "problem"—that he was temporarily short of money—the group responded with great relief and vast amounts of concern and sympathy. However, neither the therapist nor the group would have had to remain "stuck" had he been willing to utilize any of a number of techniques.

Gestalt techniques appropriate to the situation would have had members of the group in turn play the part of the critical audience and the stupid, helpless child, externalize their projections, take the role of critic and criticize the audience, "ham up" their own discomfort, etc. These procedures would have allowed them to further their own growth by reducing the internalized demands of others' expectations and to reclaim and modify their disowned disapproval, while at the same time they would be reducing the audience to "ground" and then would continue with whatever needs emerged as "figure." Suffering with another when the reasons for his suffering are not genuine or allowing him to continue with discomfort when this can be reduced is hardly humane.

A second therapist on the program specialized in behavior modification in groups. His techniques invoked persons in the group into becoming involved in such obviously insincere and artificial interactions that it came as no surprise to discover that he had carefully rehearsed the group members the night before. However, there is no need to think of suffering-with or artificial techniques as representing an either-or choice; rather, they are two undesirable extremes, between which lie many combinations of the values of potency and humanness.

The problem of symptom substitution has reappeared with the advent of behavior modification, and it has apparently become important for behavior modifiers to defend their procedures and their potency against questions as to the possibility of substitution of other unwished-for behavior and lack of permanency in the behavioral changes (see, for example, Calhoon, 1968). Part of the problem concerns the rapidity of the change—the extent to which rapid change is permanent or will be replaced with equivalent symptoms. The speed with which behavior can be changed with a reasonable degree of permanence depends on whether it is central or peripheral to personality structure and to what extent it intersects with other systems that can reapply pressure to keep it in force. In other words, the combination of speed and potency of behavior change depend on the number and strength of the props that hold up a given bit of behavior. Props may be the reinforcements of other people, catastrophic expectations on the part of the patients, ignorance, unchecked assumptions, etc. Some of these may be removed easily, especially if they are discomfort-producing and if other systems are minimally affected. The question of symptom substitution must take into account three questions: whether the symptom is replaced by another on the same level, what positive goals have occurred, and to what extent other systems have been disrupted. Let us return to the example of the boy with the stomachache presented earlier and assume that he is given medical treatment of such potency that he ceases to have stomach complaints. However, he then develops acrophobia that just as effectively keeps him at home. The physician, concerned only with the physical system, states that there is no symptom substitution, that is, there are no other medical problems and therefore the problem is solved. However, the therapist, who views the boy's main problem as avoiding school, defines the phobia as symptom substitution and proceeds to treat him by behavior modification. As a result the boy attends school but cries all the time and fails his work. Another result might be that the boy's mother, finding that she can enjoy directly controlling passively resisting men, puts such pressure on her husband that a divorce occurs. While Freud apparently cured the phobia of Little Hans, his parents did divorce (Strean, 1967). Other therapists who define the problem as success at school or the mutual satisfaction of the entire familiy would see each of these attempts as evidences of inadequate, incomplete, or inept therapy. We can continue moving up the systems ladder by hypothesizing other possibilities: what if, because of the improvement in the entire family, they come into conflict with the authoritarian school system; or the father, by deciding to leave his job, contributes to the bankruptcy of the company he worked for?

There are no final nor even clear answers to this morass, but I can offer some suggestions:

1. It is not enough to specify the symptom to be removed; it is also necessary to describe what positive functioning is expected.
2. The most important interconnecting systems should be specified and attempts made to keep disruptions to a minimum.
3. If disruptions are inevitable, the therapist should specify his value choice.

The three points above need amplification and the detailing of underlying assumptions. One is that, with very few exceptions, symptoms represent a positive as well as a negative force. Most symptoms, be they medical, individual, or social, even though painful, disturbing, and time consuming, are indicative of intersections that need to be repaired lest greater damage occur. In trying to change symptoms, we must always look to the larger system to note whether the symptom is justified. (It is possible that the school system could become so destructive that to force children's attendance would be to contribute to much more serious problems than would arise from nonattendance.) Symptoms may also have positive value, such as holding a couple together.

With our powerful Western technology we change and redo large parts of our physical environment without any appreciation of the values that we are negating and without any provisions for replacing their loss. As a result we are constantly being faced with land erosion, floods, air pollution, drops in water-tables, etc. Similarly, in therapy we are creating a technology that lets us change personality faster than we know how to solidify it or provide for the fragments left behind. If we attempt to specify what is healthy in a symptom pattern, then we will know more clearly what to leave alone.

It is also important to specify the replacement behavior for symptomatic difficulties, even though this is presently somewhat utopian. Of what value is it to remove a snake phobia—what does this contribute to living in a positive sense? Or, if we remove overt homosexual behavior, is asexuality adequate, or ability to have intercourse with randomly chosen females? Or do we aim toward the formation of a sustained, personally satisfying heterosexual involvement? Most therapists would prefer to avoid the specification of positive goals, since this involves them in clear value choices and since achievement may be embarrassingly short of the goals. It is also true that most patients request the removal of symptoms rather than specifying replacement behavior, and their goals usually change during the treatment process as additional possibilities become available. However, the therapist who does not consider the question of goals in their broader aspect becomes a mere technician, or a flunky of the values of the culture and its institutional systems.

Finally, and also ideally, if we have done our jobs thoroughly, we have not markedly disrupted any other system. This is a complicated issue, and only some of the parameters can be suggested here. It is, of course, true that growth and change are both disruptive of systems. The child will leave home in the process of growing up; changes in other systems will make an institutional administrative arrangement inadequate, causing different and expanded procedures and organization, and perhaps another kind of discomfort. We therefore have to decide whether the disruption of a system is inevitable or whether it is destructive, that is, whether it creates wounds that require extensive energy to heal, energy that could be better used for expanded growth. This question is one for Solomon; however, the therapist, even with his much more limited resources, should still have at least an awareness of his role as a system disrupter. A denial of this effect ("The only thing I do is to change a person's specific behavior") can be regarded as gross myopia. For example, consider a therapist whose patients are primarily dissatisfied housewives. In his work with them, he fosters their becoming appropriately more demanding and assertive. However, the end result is frequent marital problems and divorces, as the husbands reject their wives' demands or use them as excuses for affairs, etc. Much of this could be avoided if the therapist were willing to see couples jointly (or could modify his strong rescue needs). If the goal is to make a person less dependent, then the immediate question can be raised, less dependent upon whom? It follows that the "whom" may have some responses of his own that will likely lead to strains in the family system. If the therapist is aware of these strains, he can take steps to anticipate and deal with them.

Sometimes disruption cannot be avoided. If we are able to "decraze" a late-adolescent schizophrenic whose family refuses to be changed, then one or both parents may show psychotic symptoms themselves. (At times, one measure of change is the disruption of interrelated systems or the extent of the pressures they employ to force return to early states.) There are times when systems may well need to be abandoned: when the student should drop out of school or the worker quit his job. The therapist no longer has the luxury of avoiding the problem by decreeing that no decisions be made during therapy (life moves too quickly for this), nor can he ignore the fact that changes resulting from therapy inevitably create decision situations. Helping the patient with deciding in a given situation whether to run, fight, or compromise requires a full measure of the therapist's humanness. In general, I would prefer to maintain rather than to disrupt systems. However, this implies degrees of wisdom and power that are not yet consistently available.

When leaving a system is inevitable, the therapist can assist the patient with the reduction of unfinished business by having him in the therapy session confront, in directly spoken fantasy, the person(s) with his resentments, appreciations, regrets, and good-bys.

Finally, the therapist can predict for the patient as early as possible that system disruption may occur, allowing him to anticipate and have increased choice in the outcome. While the choice of end goals is basically the patient's, the therapist has the responsibility of anticipating and reminding the patient of as many choices as possible. There are unfortunately many conditions that reduce the number of options, and with a given patient, quite limited goals are often inevitable, given limited resources and rigid systems. The therapist should be able to accept these while being aware of further possibilities.

One of the major contributions of Gestalt therapy is the power of its techniques, which make possible the very rapid reaching of deep emotional levels. Since the other papers in this section ably describe these, no effort will be made to include them here. It should be noted, however, that having access to potent techniques presents a temptation to overuse them, and the therapist needs to be aware that he has other tasks of importance.

HUMANNESS

The therapist's contribution to the therapeutic process as a person and the importance of the genuineness and depth of the therapeutic relationship have been emphasized by a large number of therapists. Humanness, as it is used here, includes a variety of involvements: the therapist's concern for and caring about his patient on a personal and emotional level; his willingness to share himself and bring to the patient his own direct emotional responses and/or pertinent accounts of his own experiences; his ability to recognize in the patient gropings toward deepened authenticity, which need support and recognition; and his continued openness to his own growth, which serves as a model for the patient.

Some patients' needs are peripheral and can be adequately attended to by therapists with only brief or minimal involvement. But many—if not most—people were raised by families who, even while doing the best they could, taught them less about being human than they need to know. If a patient's problems stem from inadequate rearing, then the teaching of more adequate behavior is basically a process of rerearing. This requires adequate humanness in the therapist who assumes the parenting role, since he will serve extensively as a model and will have to make many value-laden decisions. This does not rule out briefer therapeutic contacts. There is a trend among some therapists who assume long-range responsibility to suggest or arrange for patients at certain stages such adjunct experiences as sensitivity training, art therapy, structural reintegration, or marathons. There is also an increasing emphasis among some behavior modifiers to consider their assignment unfinished until more adequate behavior is substituted for the symptom that is removed.

In raising children, it is the subtle learnings, attitudes, and non-verbal messages that are perhaps the most important. As the father teaches his son to fix the sled, or the mother shops for clothes with her daughter, they communicate perceptions of the child as stupid or bright, pleasant or unpleasant, likable or disgusting, and demonstrate attitudes such as interest, endurance, and enjoyment. Factual knowledge and routine bits of information are most efficiently taught by teaching machines or their equivalents, but not tolerance or curiosity, nor the value of "wasting" time.

Patients inevitably put therapists in a parental position, that is, they see them as having the secrets of living and test them in many ways to see if they will be adequate models. I tell patients, "Basically what we are doing here is seeing if I, as I am now, could have grown up in your family as you present it to me in your person, and remain sane." The patient in rapidly alternating ways involves me with his problems to see if I can respond more adequately than his parents could, and presents me with his parents' problems to see if I can find better ways of dealing with them than he was able to. For those patients for whom therapy is and becomes a central and intense experience, external living crises become relatively less important, and reenactments of growing-up crises occupy increasing attention. They progress backward through time and present their unsolved problems in a roughly reverse temporal order. Most often the final decision to accept me totally as parent comes as the result of a crisis, often following a minor mistake I made at the same time the patient is beginning to come to grips with core problems. (A somewhat limited example is given in Fagan, 1968.) The crisis is unexpected in that I can never anticipate its presentation; in retrospect it becomes apparent that the patient sets up a situation in which I am put to the test that his parents failed most badly. The crisis clearly measures my understanding of the patient's patterning, my ability to control, my potency, but most of all my humanness, since a response is unavoidable and usually must be immediate and genuine, drawing on resources that lie far below the level of techniques. I do not always pass the test. Sometimes when I do not, the patient tries again later; sometimes he gives up and adopts lesser goals; sometimes he turns to other sources of help. When I have passed, I know immediately since the patient in an unmistakable way becomes my infant and our feelings toward each other involve a kind of adoration (for example, Searles, 1965, Chap. 21). We work our way back up through developmental milestones of childhood and adolescence until the patient is as well regrown as my own resources as a parent allow. [Other descriptions of this process are given by Whitaker and Malone (1953) as the *core phase,* and by Carkhuff and Berenson (1967) as the *downward and upward stages* of therapy.] It is of course true that many therapists do not and/or cannot involve their patients to this extent, and many patients ask for assistance of a much more limited nature. However, deep personal regrowth is still experienced by those involved as either patients or therapists as the crux of therapy.

On a less intense and involved level, but still important, are those crises of living on which the therapist must respond to the patient more from this humanness than from his knowledge or techniques. These would include a severe illness, a child killed, an important goal having become unattainable, a deep rejection. Before or after dealing with those aspects that are correctable, there exists the need for bearing those parts that can only be borne. The therapist needs to know from inside himself when his presence is the most important contribution he can make to the healing process, and when his response as one human being to another is more important than any therapeutic busywork.

The events of the past few years—the civil rights struggles, student rebellions, experimental college movements, hippie communities, and the explosive growth of sensitivity training and group experiences—bespeak a level of hunger for new ways of experiencing, relating, learning, governing, etc., but they also are contributing to the development of a number of people whose experimentations are producing new levels and patterns of authenticity. If therapists fall too far behind in their own growth, they will be out of touch with an increasing proportion of the population.

The making of oneself into a whole and genuine person is probably the most difficult and painful aspect of becoming a therapist, but, for many, it is also the most valuable and important part. Many therapists who see authenticity as a primary task of the therapist fear those who, having stopped short in their own struggles with growing, substitute increased emphasis on control and potency, with a corresponding lack of regard for questions of value associated with the ability to produce personality change. The question of who controls the controllers becomes more acute as control over behavior becomes more possible. In the name of mental health, many horribly inhumane and degrading things have been done to people (Szasz, 1965b) and will no doubt continue to be done. Those who are certain of the good that they do are more to be feared than those who are more willing to admit and struggle with their own personal limitations, to share their doubts, and to express their values.

The contributions of Gestalt therapy to the humanness of the therapist come primarily in the workshop setting, which offers therapists direct experience with their own inauthenticities and avoidances. The emphasis on experiencing rather than computing, and the fostering of here-and-now awareness, pleasure, excitement, deep emotional involvement, and direct interaction seem especially designed for therapists, many of whom tend toward obsessive and depressive styles. Experiencing and observing ways in which authenticity can be distinguished from its many imitations is a valuable contribution.

Gestalt theory confronts therapists as directly as patients with reminders of the values and pleasures of living that can get pushed aside by our occupational hazards of overemphasis on work, responsibility, accomplishment, and study. Finally, in work with patients, Gestalt techniques offer a variety of ways of allowing them a rapid, deep, and authentic experience with themselves which provides an increased knowledge of what is possible as well as allowing a quick and direct "knowing" on the part of the therapist.

COMMITMENT

A number of major and minor commitments are necessary to the therapy process. The therapist commits himself to a vocation with its attendant demands for continued growth of his own understanding and ability. He also commits himself to individual patients in his work with them. Finally, he commits himself to contributing to the field as a whole by his research, writing, training of students, etc.

Commitment, or the continuing involvement and acceptance of assumed responsibilities, requires high levels of interest and energy. Interests may be maintained in a variety of ways. There are many problems that have large cognitive components, including understanding patients and constructing patterns. There is the broader task of theory addition and construction, or the long-term satisfaction of a research program. Also involving are the deep satisfaction of seeing the growth of patients, the challenge and excitement of devising new procedures and techniques, and the steady increments of the therapist's person and powers. However, no therapist can avoid boredom, depression, and doubts related to the therapeutic process and his own procedures, either for brief moments or for extended periods. If the therapist's techniques are mechanical and boring, involving him only passively or superficially, or if the interaction required creates too much anxiety, then the therapist will either be spurred to less directly central areas such as research or, unfortunately, training.

Gestalt therapy places most emphasis on the therapist's commitment to himself in terms of enhancing his involvement and excitement in the day-to-day tasks. It also provides or suggests ways for the therapist to assist himself in exploring his own boredom and doubts when they occur. In these respects it enhances both therapist and patient interest and offers ways of getting both "unstuck" when faced with the inevitable impasses.

Some final thoughts: The five tasks described in this paper will vary in their relative importance in response to many factors; the context surrounding therapy, specific requirements and limitations, the types of problems presented, and the time sequence or stage of therapy. At times the therapist will experience conflicts between two of the tasks, for example, between control and humanness. As the emphasis shifts from task to task, to some extent the image of the therapist shifts, in a way that, with much magnification, parallels the popular stereotypes of the therapist as the mind reader who knows all, as the hypnotist who can control persons against their will, as the magician who has a collection of magic tricks, as the loving Big Daddy or Mommie, and as the faithful, patient family retainer.

In summary, many requirements are made of the therapist as he sets out to assist another person. These have been discussed under five headings: patterning, control, potency, humanness, and commitment. The therapist's response to these involves him as a complete person, including his intellectual knowledge and cognitive abilities, his interpersonal effectiveness, his emotional awareness and personal sensitivity, his values and interests, and his experience in living. Certainly one of the continued challenges and fascinations of therapy is the variety of demands that it places on the therapist and its ability to require and evoke from him an involvement and utilization of all his resources.

References

Berne, E. *Games people play*. New York: Grove Press, 1964.

Bion, W. R. *Experience in groups, and other papers*. New York: Basic Books, 1961.

Bugental, J. F. T. *The search for authenticity: An existential-analytic approach to psychotherapy*. New York: Holt, Rinehart & Winston, 1965.

Calhoon, D. D. Symptom substitution and the behavioral therapies: A reappraisal. *Psychological Bulletin,* 1968, *69,* 149–156.

Carkhuff, R. R., & Berenson, B. G. *Beyond counseling and therapy.* New York: Holt, Rinehart & Winston, 1967.

Fagan, J. Message from mother. *Psychotherapy: Theory, Research and Practice,* 1968, *5,* 21–23.

Goulding, R. *Introductory lectures in transactional analysis.* Atlanta, Ga., 1967.

Greenwald, H. Treatment of the psychopath. *Voices,* 1967, *3* (1), 50–61.

Haley, J. The art of psychoanalysis. In S. I. Hayakawa (Ed.), *Our language and our world.* New York: Harper & Brothers, 1959.

Haley, J. Control in brief psychotherapy. *Archives of General Psychiatry,* 1961, *4,* 139–153. (a)

Haley, J. Control in psychotherapy with schizophrenics. *Archives of General Psychiatry,* 1961, *5,* 340–353. (b)

Haley, J. *Strategies of psychotherapy.* New York: Grune & Stratton. 1963.

Haley, J. & Hoffman, L. *Techniques of family therapy.* New York: Basic Books, 1968.

Langsley, D. G., Pittman, F. S., Machotka, P., & Flomenhaft, K. Family crisis therapy—results and implications. *Family Process,* 1968, *7,* 145–158.

Rogers, C. R. *Client-centered therapy.* Boston: Houghton Mifflin, 1951.

Rogers, C. R. (Ed.) *The therapeutic relationship and its impact: A study of psychotherapy with schizophrenics.* Madison, Wisc.: University of Wisconsin Press, 1967.

Rosen, J. N. *Direct analysis: Selected papers.* New York: Grune & Stratton, 1953.

Schwartz, L. J. Treatment of the adolescent psychopath—theory and case report. *Psychotherapy: Theory, Research and Practice,* 1967, *4,* 133–137.

Searles, H. F. *Collected papers on schizophrenia and related subjects.* New York: International Universities Press, 1965.

Strean, H. S. A family therapist looks at "Little Hans." *Family Process,* 1967, *6,* 227–234.

Szasz, T. S. *The ethics of psychoanalysis: The theory and method of autonomous psychotherapy.* New York: Basic Books, 1965. (a)

Szasz, T. S. *Psychiatric justice.* New York: Macmillan, 1965. (b)

Truax, C. B., & Carkhuff, R. R. *Toward effective counseling and psychotherapy: Training and practice.* Chicago: Aldine, 1967.

Whitaker, C. A., & Malone, T. P. *The roots of psychotherapy.* New York: Blakiston, 1953.

chapter 2

AN INTRODUCTION TO GESTALT TECHNIQUES

John B. Enright

Gestalt therapy has been (and is still being) developed by Frederick S. Perls out of three quite distinct sources and influences: psychoanalysis, particularly as modified by the early Wilhelm Reich; European phenomenology-existentialism; and Gestalt psychology. Perls's *Gestalt Therapy* presents the theory of personality structure and growth from which the therapy can be derived, and a series of experiments in self-awareness to be directly used by the reader. However, the range, variety, and power of the techniques developed by Perls and his associates deserve more extensive description, both within a general framework of purpose and procedure and in terms of specific types of interventions. This paper will concentrate primarily on therapeutic goals and strategy, with occasional brief discussion of specific tactics and techniques.

In the Gestalt point of view, the healthy organism-in-its-environment is constantly attending to matters of importance to its maintenance or survival. These matters of importance are organism-environment *transactions* that keep or restore equilibrium or smooth functioning. "Attending" here does not refer to a conscious state but to a behavioral focusing of parts of the organism toward relevant parts of the environment, with muscular tonus, sensory tracking, etc. Most of this directed behavior takes place at the shifting boundary of organism and environment, where that which is novel and alien in the environment is contacted and made part of the organism (for example, food is ingested and assimilated or words are heard and understood).

In human beings, *awareness* develops where novelty and complexity of transaction are greatest, and the most possibilities (for good or ill) exist. Awareness seems to facilitate maximum efficiency by concentrating all the organism's abilities on the most complex, possibility-loaded situations.

In this oversimplified account, awareness is a state of consciousness that develops spontaneously when organismic attention becomes focused on some particular region of the organism-environment contact boundary at which an especially important and complex transaction is occurring. If this view is accepted, a disarmingly simple definition of psychological malfunctioning becomes possible. Something is going wrong when awareness does *not* develop at this region of complex interaction. A correspondingly simple theory of therapy follows, as a first approximation to a statement of the goal of Gestalt therapy: therapy consists of the *reintegration of attention and awareness.*

The task of the therapist is to help the patient overcome the barriers (of which more later) that block awareness, and to let nature take its course (that is, awareness develop) so he can function with all his abilities. Note that the therapist in this view does not help directly with the transaction—he does not help solve the problem—but helps reestablish the conditions under which the patient can best use his own problem-solving abilities.

From this simple formulation follows a considerable amount of what the Gestalt therapist does in practice. He watches for splits in attention and awareness, for evidence that focused organismic attention is developing outside of awareness. Though the patient may be talking about some problem, he is also from moment to moment sensorily registering and motorically doing much else. Though his awareness is generally concentrated on the verbal content, he also may be gazing into space, fiddling with his hands, shifting around, smiling—at times in congruence with verbal content, at times perhaps not. His voice also varies in quality, sometimes matching the shifts in verbal content, sometimes not. In addition to the "intended" content of his words, there is also the rich and subtle texture of imagery and metaphor, the selection of verb voice, mode, and tense, the shifts in pronouns, etc. These serve as the linguistic "ground" that modifies and enriches the lexical meaning of his words. All this bears relationship to the patient's difficulties in living an organismically satisfying life. He is showing us from moment to moment and in detail just how he avoids being in full contact with his current actuality—how he avoids awareness of ongoing matters of organismic importance to him.

When the patient is communicating well verbally, and his other ongoing activities are minimal or congruent, I listen. At those times I assume his awareness to be integrated with his organismic attention, and thus he is doing nothing that I as a psychotherapist can help him with; his problems are his, and he is working in them effectively at the moment. In a family or group, members are in good contact with each other at such times, communicating well and dealing with their interpersonal problems effectively. My task begins when these other "unconscious" activities begin to stand out in the total gestalt and vie with the verbal content. I then encourage the patient(s) to devote some attention to these other activities, asking him to describe what he is doing, seeing, feeling. I make no interpretations but simply draw awareness to these phenomena, and let him make of them what he will. Quite often, if my timing is good and my perception of increasing saliency accurate, the patient can make quite good sense of these and gain in awareness of what he is doing. Some brief clinical examples may be helpful here.

A woman in individual therapy is going over, in a very complaining voice, some examples of how she was recently mistreated by her mother-in-law. I am impressed in her account by her lack of awareness of how much she invited this, and how she underperceives her capacity to interrupt this behavior but said nothing. My attention is caught by a rapid repetitive movement of her hand against her other arm, though I can't make the movement out.

T.: What are you doing with your hand?
P.: (*slightly startled*) Uh, making a cross.
T.: A cross?
P.: Yes (*pause*).
T.: What might you do with a cross?
P.: Well, I certainly hung myself on one this weekend, didn't I?

She returns to her account, but with more awareness of her martyr attitude and its contribution to events.

A couple in marital therapy are going over their problems rather repetitiously and fruitlessly. The wife is staring past me quite fixedly.

T.: What are you looking at?
W.: The tape recorder.
T.: Can you describe what you are seeing?
W.: Yes. It's just going round and round and round.
T.: Round and round?
W.: Yes.
T.: Is anything else going round and round?
H. & W.: (*simultaneously and rather impatiently*) *We* certainly are.

They return to their discussion, but more fully aware of their sterile circularity, and they begin to take more productive steps to break out of it.

An intellectualizing male graduate student in group therapy announces blandly to no one in particular, "I have difficulty in relating to people." In the ensuing silence, he glances briefly at the attractive nurse who was cotherapist. The therapist immediately asked, "Who *here* do you have trouble relating to?" The student is able to name the nurse, and spends a fruitful five minutes exploring his mixed frustration, attraction, and anger focused on this desirable but inaccessible woman.

A paranoid woman in her first group therapy meeting on the ward begins by telling in a flat, affectless voice that her husband tried to poison her. She continues to enumerate her delusional complaints, but also mentions a severe pain in the back of her neck. Asked to describe this, she says that it is as though she had been struck a judo blow and also indicates that her husband knows judo. Able now to say that she feels as though her husband had actually struck her, she can, when questioned, soon begin to talk about ways in which her husband symbolically hurt her. Soon she is telling the group, with appropriate tears and anger, how her husband slights and ignores her, and flirts with other women. Temporarily she has abandoned the paranoid solution to her problems.

A constricted, overinhibited man is tapping his finger on the table while a woman in the group talks on and on. Asked if he has anything to comment about what the woman is saying, he denies much concern with it but continues the tapping. He is asked then to intensify the tapping, to tap louder and more vigorously, and to continue until he feels more fully what he is doing. His anger mounts quickly and in a minute or so he is pounding the table and expressing vehemently his disagreement with the woman. He declares that she is "just like my wife," but in addition to this historical perspective, he has had an experiential glimpse of his excessive control of strong assertive feelings and the possibilities of more immediate and hence less violent expression of them.

There are several important characteristics of the therapeutic interventions described above that attempt to help the patient integrate attention and awareness. (*a*) The intervention builds on actual present behavior—some *present* concern of the organism is involved, although neither patient nor therapist may have any idea what it is when the intervention is made, and it may turn out to be quite unrelated to the verbal material concurrently expressed. (*b*) Ideally, and usually, the intervention is noninterpretive. I ask what is going on or what he is doing; where we go from there depends on the patient's answer. If he makes connection with the verbal material or achieves some understanding of what he is doing, he has done it for himself in his own language. If he denies any connection or experiences nothing in his behavior, that is up to him; typically I let the matter drop. My timing was bad or he was not ready. If I push for a response or give my interpretation, he may only mobilize more defenses against me. If the behavior is important, it will happen again. (*c*) A third characteristic of this style of intervention is that it continually operates to enhance and expand the patient's sense of responsibility for his own behavior. Responsibility here means not the broad sense of "social responsibility," but rather the feeling that "I, here and now, am aware of doing thus and so." (However, I feel that true responsibility in the broader sense is rooted in this feeling of being the actual agent.) Thus, throughout the course of therapy, whatever the content, the patient is learning to do for himself, and to face indecision and make choices—on a small but increasing scale.

The questions that introduce these interventions are almost exclusively "what" and "how" questions, seldom "what for" or "why." Most people most of the time don't fully know *what* they are doing, and it is a considerable therapeutic contribution if the patient can achieve a vivid and ongoing awareness of his moment-to-moment behavior and surroundings. In a sense, the achievement of such full awareness is all that therapy need do; when a person feels fully and vividly what he is doing, his concern about why usually fades away. If he does remain interested, he is in a good position to work it out for himself.

In keeping with this bias of Gestalt therapy in favor of 'what" and "how" questions, I will now consider in more detail some of the ways in which areas of self-functioning are kept out of awareness, and some of the consequences of this blocking. Four ways will be considered: retroflection, desensitization, introjection, and projection. All four can be seen functioning from moment to moment in the here and now to block awareness of current behavior, or as repetitive residuals of earlier attempts to avoid awareness. A brief discussion may leave the false impression that these only rephrase existing concepts, and certainly there is extensive overlap with related concepts from psychoanalysis and general psychiatry. The difference in emphasis is often quite subtle and would require a fairly extensive discussion to clarify.

Projection. The individual attributes disowned aspects of himself to others, becoming hypersensitive or critical of minor manifestations. There is perhaps more emphasis in Gestalt therapy than in psychiatry on the less pathological forms of projection in which the individual does not distort reality seriously but shows his overconcern only in his perceptual selectivity of certain phenomena from the whole range of his surroundings.

Retroflection. An impulse or idea is rooted in organismic sensorimotor tension, shaped partly by inner drives and focused on environmental events or objects. Retroflection describes the general process of negating, holding back, or balancing the impulse tension by additional, opposing sensorimotor tension. The concept includes most of what is often referred to as repression and inhibition, and emphasizes the *how* of the processes involved. Since the net result of all this canceled-out muscular tension is zero—no overt movement—there is no particular increase in activity at the contact boundary, and awareness does not develop. Later, perhaps, since there is increased activity at the points of muscular opposition, awareness may develop there as pain or discomfort. This process of retroflection can be transitory or chronic. The cry of distress begins with moistening of the eyes and a characteristic facial expression; the "stiff upper lip" and the literal holding (squeezing) back of tears constitute the retroflection. This can last a moment before the tears break through or (as Tomkins, 1963, describes so vividly) a lifetime.

Perls's debt to Wilhelm Reich is most clear in the development of this concept. Reich's "character armor" is chronic retroflection. It is important to note that the organism is expending energy in maintaining the tension of both the impulse and resistance, and both are quite typically alienated from the self and awareness. Both need to be "reclaimed" in therapy and made available for satisfying, constructive use.

Desensitization. This is the sensory analog to motoric retroflection. Scotomata, visual blurring, chronic "not hearing," sensory dullness, frigidity, etc., are equal in importance to retroflection in the blocking of awareness. They are, however, more dependent on verbal report and hence less accessible to direct observation and study than motoric phenomena.

Introjections. These consist of complex, integrated ways of behaving or being, adopted wholesale by the developing organism from significant others *without assimilation or integration with the self.* They correspond quite closely to Berne's (1961) "parent" or "exteropsychic" ego states. They can be detected by the repeated concurrence of a certain voice quality, type of verbal content, and gesture-posture style, and by the similarity with which others respond to this unified complex of behavior. The details of the process by which these introjects are taken in are complex and unnecessary for this discussion. Our interest here is primarily in the role they play in current life. There they are the chief actors in the endless self-nagging and inner argument between the "ideal" and "real" self in which so many people fritter away their lives. They also clutter up interpersonal relations, when the self plays out one of these roles with significant others or projects one of them onto another person. Introjects are one of the main transmitters of pathology across the generations. An individual who may have successfully minimized his use of introjects in other areas of his life still may activate them when he functions as a parent with his own children.

Insofar as the individual relies on any of these means for the transitory or chronic blocking of awareness, he leaves himself with vast areas alienated and inaccessible, interfering with rather than facilitating the flow of life. He feels—and in a sense is—weak and divided, pushed and pulled by forces outside himself. His behavior tends to be graceless and awkward; breathing and vocal expression are crippled. And with so little energy left over to live with, a great deal of "unfinished business" piles up.

Unfinished business is perhaps the major consequence of the blocking of awareness. Need cycles cannot be completed; tension is aroused but not reduced; affect mounts and is unexpressed. The flow of behavior is clogged with unexpressed action; little new can happen in the ensuing constriction and frustration. The individual becomes "hung up" on the unexpressed; life slows down into despair and boredom with lack of autonomy, spontaneity, and intimacy. The neurotic's life is not a happy one, even if he does not happen to develop one of the specialized symptoms such as phobias, obsessions, or anxiety; it remains merely gray and unfulfilled. Frequently his conscious ego is not in very good touch with what is wrong, and his verbal account of his "problems" is often quite wide of the mark. He has successfully distracted himself from even knowing where he hurts, and his "problem" or "presenting complaint" is not the meaningful place to start therapy. Quite often he would be only too happy to talk indefinitely and abstractly about The Problem, keeping "it" safely at a distance. If he is trained as a patient, he may come in ready to ruminate his current fantasies about his childhood, with the same distancing intent and result.

Fortunately, the general strategy of Gestalt therapy does not depend on the patient's accuracy in self-report. We simply tell him, in effect, to sit down and start living, then note where and how he fails. The therapeutic value we implicitly ask him to accept is that he will probably be more effective and comfortable in his life in the long run if he is more fully aware of what he is doing from moment to moment, and if he can accept responsibility for this behavior. He may have to accept this on faith for a short time, but we hope very soon to demonstrate the advantages of this orientation directly and concretely.

In this situation the organism will immediately turn in some way to whichever of its store of unfinished business is pressing and more or less relevant to the current situation. His techniques for blocking awareness will immediately come into play: he will begin to show in his projections, tension, and dissociated activity the portions of his self that are alienated and inaccessible. The therapist can choose the most salient of these with which to begin. I have become impressed with the importance and probable centrality of the *very first* opening gambit—verbal or not—of the patient. Where he sits, at whom he glances, the sigh, the smile, the posture, the idiosyncratic image in his opening remark—anything he says before he formally begins to talk about The Problem—all are rich leads to the most deeply involving material he is likely to be able to get to, if the way can be found to use this material nonthreateningly.

The beginning can be—indeed should be—some trivial surface event, such as a smile at the therapist. When this is expressed more fully and awarely, the patient is ready to go on to the next, slightly more involving fact that he is, now that he thinks about it, also a little angry at the nice therapist. And so on, through layers of resistance and impulse—each one dwelt on as long as necessary, and hopefully not left behind until the energy invested in it is available for use, and the patient is not too anxious about the next step into the unknown and unexpressed. Resistances are not "overcome," but identified with and made one's own. Affect or impulse are not balanced or blocked in expression, but encouraged into more intense and full expression, finishing the business, and leaving decks cleared for new action. No attempt is made to keep the patient on any "topic" as verbally presented; instead, a systematic and aggressive attempt is made to keep him in constant contact with *what he is doing*. He is then encouraged to do whatever this is as fully and completely as he can, with growing awareness of what he is doing. If he blocks himself from doing it, we then turn attention to how he is blocking himself and encourage fuller and more aware expression of this. The therapist spends as little time and energy as possible speculating on what is likely to emerge from each step the patient takes but instead concentrates on timing of the steps and listening as fully as possible to what the patient is doing. This is perhaps the most significant gain of noninterpretative therapy. The therapist is liberated from his endless fantasies about what is going to emerge from the patient in the next few minutes (with associated anxiety about whether he is right or wrong) and instead can simply listen and help the patient find his own way through the pauses and blocks.

The basic assumption of this therapeutic approach is that patients deal adequately with their own life problems—if they know what they are and can bring all their abilities into action to solve them. Our task is to unblock awareness by helping patients relax their retroflected energies, restore sensitivity, assimilate introjects, and change projection into direct expression. Once in good touch with their real concerns and their real environment; they are on their own.

Gestalt Techniques in Group and Family Therapy

So far, an effort has been made to present techniques of Gestalt therapy that are generally applicable to all modes of therapy: individual, group, and family. Some of the techniques and tactics presented can be more powerful when we ask the patient to sit down and start living in a group with new people he must learn to deal with; or to sit down with his family and become aware of interactions with these significant but frustrating others. In a group, abstract problems can more quickly and readily be brought to earth. A patient who complains that he can't speak up and criticize his wife might be asked to address a critical remark to each group member present, thus experiencing immediately his difficulty instead of talking *about* it. A patient who claims to have an "inferiority complex" might be greeted with the request to indicate to whom in the present group she feels inferior, and how. With many more people available, the range of unfinished business that can be quite readily contacted is much greater. More people provide more screens on which projections can be cast, and the work of reclaiming and expressing them can be more easily done. For example, a patient who comments that another patient is "looking contemptuously at the group" might be asked himself to "try out" looking contemptuously at the group to see if he can make contact with his own feelings of contempt, and express them directly instead of through projective oversensitivity.

In addition to the enhancing effects of getting several patients together, there are certain techniques that are specific to people in a group. In addition to the therapeutic value of awareness and responsibility already mentioned, we ask the group or family patient to accept another group-specific value: that in the long run he will probably deal more effectively and better with people around him if he is direct with them and listens to them with respect for them as individuals. Again, he must briefly accept this on faith, but we hope soon to demonstrate its validity concretely. In essence, the techniques about to be presented all follow from this value assumption and are simply ways of implementing this belief about human relations. The goal we set for the patients as they sit down together in a group or family is an "I-thou" relationship in which each person is aware, responsible, and direct in his own communications and listens as fully as possible to the other person as an equal.

The first technique implementing this point of view about human relations is to ask as quickly and fully as possible, in all interactions that take place in the group, that people speak directly to each other without use of the third person. A is discouraged from making some comment about B to the therapist and is asked rather to rephrase his comment in some form directly to B. This sounds simple, almost trivial, but in practice it is very powerful. Patients often respond to this request first by saying that it is too simple to bother with, or that it doesn't matter; but when they try, they go on rebelling strongly against it. The affect mobilized by such direct confrontation is very different from that which can be dissipated indirectly in the third-person comment. Typically, a patient has considerable difficulty in making very much of a direct statement to another. The most common result of an attempt at directness is that ambivalence immediately becomes apparent, usually nonverbally, and the "simple" statement immediately turns out to be very complicated indeed. This ambivalence and difficulty with directness then become the focus of therapy. For example, a patient may attempt a critical statement to another, and look away from the other in the middle of the statement or interrupt it with a smile. We might ask him then what he was looking away from, or to put the smile into words. If he says he was looking away from the other's angry expression, he can get immediate feedback, and perhaps go on to find out that the anger he saw was his own, projected. As he gropes to put his placating smile into words, he becomes more aware of how he blocks and weakens his own assertiveness. As he succeeds in expressing the placation in words, he is then open to the further possibility of becoming aware of how his placating is tinged with contempt toward the other for being fooled by it, and is itself complex and ambivalent. The advantages of directness—the more immediate and fuller feedback from the other and the expansion of one's own awareness—are experienced almost immediately in this approach. Since the individuals are engaged face to face with each other in this small-scale encounter, they learn these advantages in the most direct way possible, with the greatest likelihood of carry-over into their outside lives.

A second technique to encourage the patient's awareness of responsibility for his own position is to discourage questions. A question from one patient to another usually serves either or both of two purposes. For one, it says in effect, "you speak, not me," and thus is a way of avoiding the questioner's participation. Second, almost all questions turn out to be implied statements, usually critical, about the other person. "Why did you do that?" almost always means "You shouldn't have done that," "I don't like it that you did that," or something to that effect. A question is almost never an uncomplicated request for information. As much as possible, depending on the level of the group, the Gestalt therapist will insist that a question be rephrased as a statement before the other person is asked to "answer" it. Then, since the statement is no longer masked as a question, B is released from the necessity of "answering" it (that is, defending or justifying himself) and can more easily give his total response to A.

The second therapeutic value of the group—listening to others—can be implemented in a variety of ways. I often question the intent of an interruption. If people seem to be drifting off, I will ask if it is becoming hard to listen, thus getting the group to consider simultaneously its obligation to listen and the speaker's obligation to be worth listening to. A game of hostile and unproductive "verbal ping-pong" might be interrupted by insisting that each participant paraphrase the other to the other's satisfaction before being permitted to give his own response.

The details of technique vary, but the strategy is always to keep a steady, gentle pressure toward the direct and responsible I-thou orientation, keeping the focus of awareness on the difficulties the patients experience in doing this, and helping them find their own ways through these difficulties.

This strategy of Gestalt therapy is most effective in family therapy. Family therapy differs from individual-focused therapy in that the patient's central presenting life problem is itself brought into the consulting room. The patient does not have to increase his awareness in relation to some stranger, then figure out later how to use this to modify his relations to significant others. His significant others are present with him. In a very real sense, the family is the patient and can work on its *joint* unfinished business. The unsaid accusations, the unexpressed guilt, love, and resentment that are clogging up the flow of interfamily feeling must be expressed by the family, in its own language, at its own pace. The therapist's task is again to keep turning the focus of awareness on the difficulties that stand in the way of maintaining the I-thou orientation.

Key Issues in Therapy

There are a number of issues on which any theory of therapy must take some stand. The position of Gestalt therapy on some of these could be induced from the above account, but it might be helpful to make these stands explicit. Six issues will be discussed: (1) the actual therapeutic agent as seen by Gestalt therapy and the concept of the mentally healthy person that follows from this position; (2) the criteria for termination of Gestalt therapy; (3) the range of applicability of the therapy; (4) the use of dreams; (5) the place of the therapist as a person in the technique; and (6) the place of the past in a here-and-now therapy.

Awareness, consciousness, insight, and the mentally healthy person. The theoretical and therapeutic core of Gestalt therapy is *awareness.* This is essentially an undefined term referring to a particular kind of immediate experience, but it is possible to attempt some verbal description and distinguish it from other states of consciousness. Awareness develops *with* and is integrally *part of* an organismic-environmental transaction. It includes thinking and feeling, but it is always based on current perception of the current situation.

Much of the usual "content" of consciousness for many people is a flow of fantasy-imagery and subvocal speech (thinking) that is *not* deeply rooted in ongoing behavior, but only partially and tangentially related to it. Occasionally this fantasy-thinking is focused, in necessary anticipatory problem-solving or working on some unfinished business that is important but not currently represented in the environment. More frequently this detached thinking-imagery is a more unfocused, pointless, dreamlike reverie, obsessing about, without particularly working on, unfinished business and serving mainly to distract and attenuate awareness of the actual.

The difference between awareness and this unfocused reverie is most clear in the process of eating. Awareness of eating would include the appearance, smell, and taste of the food; the kinesthetic sense of the destruction of the food though chewing and swallowing; and the associated affects of pleasure or disgust. In fact, of course, most people while eating are engaged primarily in some sort of reverie. They engage, perhaps, in revenge fantasies about some recent slight, a rerun of the latest Giants' game, or even fantasies about what they are going to eat for dessert in a few minutes—anything rather than the actual ongoing organismic activity. Many people clutter up their lives almost constantly with this internal noise of pointless and only shallowly gratifying fantasy. Since it is not substantially gratifying and does not successfully resolve any unfinished business, its consequences are to make the actual ongoing behavior (in this case, eating) less satisfying and to create more unfinished business. For example, consider an obsessive student who interrupts his studying with fantasies of the evening's date. When evening comes, and studying is not completed or well done, he ruins his date worrying about studying.

No implication is intended that in healthy life awareness is particularly big, grand, or ever-exciting. It is simply there, flowing along with behavior. In therapy, however, when awareness develops where it has been previously blocked, it does tend to be accompanied by a sense of release of tension and a feeling of increase in energy. The experience is in a sense pleasurable. Even when the developing awareness is of a painful affect such as mourning or anger, it is accompanied by a feeling of "I want this; I'm glad it's happening even though it is painful." This gratifying aspect of therapeutic awareness is crucial since it is the internal rewarding and motivating factor that permits and encourages the patient to press on even into very painful feelings.

Awareness needs particularly to be distinguished from introspection. In introspection, the self is split; part is "looking at" another part as object, self-consciously. Awareness is the whole self, conscious of that to which the organism is attending. Introspection is effortful, forced concentration; awareness is spontaneous concentration on that which is exciting and of interest. Introspection, being relatively detached from ongoing total organismic concern and being out of touch with the actual environment, can never discover anything very new, but only rearrange and rehash the verbally remembered and hence unnourishing past. Awareness, being in contact with the current environment and organism, always includes something refreshingly new. Genuine awareness is always a little bit of a surprise since neither the organism nor the environment is ever quite the same. (A person who claims that an experience is "the same" as a previous one is telling us that he is actually replaying a fantasy rather than attending with awareness to his actual experience.) Awareness as it develops in therapy almost always follows a sense of taking a chance or taking a step into the unknown—of groping to say the unsayable or beginning something without being sure of the ending. When this experience is not present, almost certainly the "insight" being presented is a sterile rehash rather than an expansion of awareness.

It would be impossible in the scope of this introduction fully to articulate this fundamental concept of awareness with its analog in psychoanalysis (*insight*), but a brief consideration of their relation might be helpful. Quite early in the history of psychoanalysis, its theoreticians and therapists became concerned that insight did *not* always produce the expected and desired therapeutic changes. One insight would seem to work; another remarkably similar-seeming one would lead nowhere. In the attempt to account for this difference a distinction was introduced between *intellectual* and *emotional* insight—the latter being the insight that "worked." The Gestalt therapist would say that the "emotional" insight (whatever its verbal form: past, present, or future) was based on an expansion of awareness of an ongoing organism-environment relationship with its associated positive affect and sense of discovery, while the "intellectual" insight lacked this crucial rootedness in the actual. This is an oversimplification of a very complex matter, but hints at the relationship of these two central concepts.

A complete theory of therapy should include some image of the healthy functioning it purports to help people achieve. Gestalt therapy considers the mentally healthy person as one in whom awareness can develop without blocking, wherever his organismic attention is drawn. Such a person can experience his own needs and the environmental possibilities fully and clearly from moment to moment, accepting both as given and working toward creative compromises. He still has his full share of inner conflicts of needs and environmental frustrations, but, being in close touch with these developing needs and the environment, he is capable of achieving reasonably adequate solutions quickly and does not magnify his real problems with fantasy elaborations.

Since he is carrying around much less of a filtering

cloud of thought-fantasies to obscure the world, his sensual world is vivid and colorful, and his interpersonal world relatively uncontaminated with projections and unreal expectations. He can perceive and respond to others much more as they are and become from moment to moment, rather than as fixed stereotypes. He has a clear sense of the relative importance of things and can do what has to be done to finish situations. Since unfinished business does not pile up, he is free to do and be quite fully and intensely whatever he is doing or being, and people around him often report a sense of his being much more *with* them when he is with them. Seeing people reasonably clearly and without excessive fantasy, it is easy for him to be quite direct with others and appreciate them for what they are. Again, he has his share of conflicts with others, but he can resolve those conflicts that are resolvable, and let go of those that are not. (And he can usually tell the difference!) He is self-respecting in every sense, including an appreciation and enjoyment of his body with consequent physical grace.

Criteria for termination of therapy. A central characteristic of Gestalt therapy is that the patient as much as possible carries out his own therapy, with the therapist standing by as observer-commentator and occasional guide. The patient as much as possible makes his own interpretations, formulates his own direct statements to others, and achieves his own awareness. We see this not as thrusting the patient's responsibility for his own behavior onto him, but rather as refusing to permit him to thrust it onto us. It rightfully is his, and we do him a disservice if we do something for him, depriving him of the learning experience and enhancement of ego functions consequent on his doing it himself.

It is quite consistent with this general orientation to ask the patient as quickly as possible to take over the responsibility for deciding to continue therapy, for deciding what he is getting from it and whether he values this sufficiently to continue. We quickly show him what we have to offer; he experiences immediately some rewards of increased awareness and evaluates for himself if this is valuable and meaningful to him.

This can be implemented in many ways. I ask individuals and families almost from the first meeting if they would like another session, and end almost every group session by asking the members how they feel it went. Doubts about progress—verbally or nonverbally expressed—become the focus of discussion, and the patient is asked in effect what he intends to do about his discontents.

Not surprisingly, many patients find this request to make their own decision rather startling. It often brings quite precipitously into the foreground some otherwise quite well-concealed fantasies about magical cures and what the therapist is going to "do for" him. In the very process of exploring these, the patient can sometimes get glimmers of his own potential strength and capacity for self-direction. Issues of responsibility, choice, goals of therapy, and autonomy often then become the beginning foci of therapy.

The whole course of therapy goes differently when termination is a central issue from the beginning. The patient cannot reasonably terminate without evaluating his progress and cannot do this without being aware of his goals. Goals can—indeed, usually do—change, but the danger of both patient and therapist losing sight of goals and drifting is minimized. Occasionally there are practical consequences of this approach in the form of quite irregular schedules as some patients, finding it very difficult to say directly, "I want an appointment next week," come more sporadically. Although these patients will have fewer contacts over a given time span, perhaps for them this is best.

Range of applicability. It is clear from the above discussion that Gestalt therapy in pure culture is not for every patient. Basically it is designed for someone who is dissatisfied with some way he is, and is willing to expend some effort to be different—or to become more content the way he is. Many of the specific techniques and principles can be applied to less willing patients—children, some psychotics, and some character disorders—but it is beyond the scope of this introduction to discuss the modifications necessary for such applications.

Therapeutic use of dreams. Since Freud's brilliant work, any system of therapy must provide either a way of working with dreams or a justification for avoiding them. Gestalt therapy meets this challenge with a totally noninterpretive approach that permits the patient to progress at his own pace and find his own meaning in his dreams. Every image in the dream, whether human, animal, vegetable, or mineral, is taken to represent an alienated portion of the self. By reexperiencing and retelling the dream over and over again in the present tense, from the standpoint of each image, the patient can begin to reclaim these alienated fragments, accept them, live with them, and express them more appropriately.

For example, a restless, domineering, manipulative

woman dreamed of walking down a crooked path in a forest of tall straight trees. Asking her *to become* one of these trees, makes her feel more serene and deeply rooted. By taking these feelings back into her current life, she then experienced both the lack of them and the possibilities of achieving them. *Becoming* the crooked path, her eyes filled with tears as she experienced more intensely the devious crookedness of her own life, and again, the possibilities of straightening out a little if she chose.

The role of the therapist is simply to suggest the order in which the images might be contacted, usually from the less to the more vivid ones. He also helps deal with the resistances—the tendencies to talk about and interpret instead of entering the experience of the image—and occasionally suggests when to carry the dream images and feelings back into the context of the patient's current existence.

Place of the "therapist-as-a-person." A major issue between current theories of therapy is: Is the therapist a technician or a person? Does he greet the patient's gambit with a professional technique, or with his own spontaneous human response? In the ranks of Gestalt therapists, I have encountered both extremes, for Gestalt therapy takes no stand on this. Anything goes, if it contributes to the patient's expansion of awareness. I have found myself moving slowly but steadily in the direction of more open revelation of my own feelings of boredom, pleasure, annoyance, embarrassment, etc. Strictly speaking, this is still technique. If the patient is talking in a monotone, staring at the floor, and I am getting a little bored, I might ask him if he is aware of his voice, or what he is looking at. I might also help him to the same awareness of his withdrawal by commenting that I am finding it hard to listen closely to him. Although this is indeed my human response, it is hardly spontaneous if I pause to decide between these approaches! In any case, I steer clear of the presumptuous interpretation, "You are trying to bore me." This may well be true, but I want him to discover it himself if it is so, and I want to set a model of responsibility by stating only what I *know* to be true—that I am finding it hard to listen.

Place of the past in a here-and-now therapy. Any here-and-now system of therapy must have some way of dealing, both in theory and practice, with the past. In theory, after all, the past "caused" the present. In practice, the patient often comes in fully expecting—in fact bound and determined—to deal with the past. This is especially true now that the popularization of psychoanalysis is pretty much complete.

Frequently a preference for talking about the past (either on the part of the patient or therapist) is a maneuver to maintain distance from potentially threatening current concerns. The patient would rather blame her mean daddy for past deprivations than upbraid the therapist here and now for withholding the here-and-now goodies (advice, cure, insight, or whatever). The therapist would far rather talk about the patient's "incestuous fantasies" than about her here-and-now coy flirtatiousness—and perhaps his own growing response to it. So a conspiracy of verbiage about the past is quite often purely defensive and distancing, and should be short-circuited as rapidly as possible.

At times, however, the patient presents some past

events in a genuinely involved and concerned manner. At these times I respect his concern and listen. I still view this language of the past as a fable wherein the patient is telling me allegorically about some present concern, but at least the discourse is concernful rather than defensive. I treat the material very much as a dream, listening in it for the parallels to the patient's current existence, and trying to help make the transition when appropriate. Almost never do I find it fruitful to inquire into the details about "what really happened." The fable then turns into a "just-so" story that can be used to prove anything the patient wants to prove.

This tendency to limit the discourse to the present is feasible only because in Gestalt therapy we listen to the *total communication* rather than the strictly verbal. The relevant past *is* present here and now; if not in words, then in some bodily tension and attention that can hopefully be brought into awareness. It is impossible to overstress the importance of this point. For a purely verbal therapy to remain in the here and now would be irresponsible and disastrous. It is only the aggressive, systematic, and constant effort to bring the patient's total communication into his awareness that permits a radical concentration on the here and now.

This is an appropriate place to take up the fundamental psychoanalytic concepts of repetition-compulsion and transference, to articulate these with the concept of unfinished business, and to discuss the Gestalt therapy alternatives to the use of these concepts. This is again a complex and subtle task, and this presentation will only atempt to suggest the nature of the relationships of these concepts. Gestalt therapy does not deny that the hand of the past has, to a large extent, shaped the present, but in addition it points out two facts: one, that the past-shaped present nevertheless does exist in its own right, with all the relevant past actually present in some form; the other, that there is always something a little new in this current instance of the repeated compulsion or in this recurrence of the transference relationship. The organism may be rigid, but the environment at least is always a little different. This particular here-and-now relationship may be 99 percent determined by transference but nevertheless have a 1 percent leeway for creative variability, since the therapist *is not* the father and cannot be "exactly like" him.

Gestalt therapy attempts to expand the 1 percent and draw the patient's awareness to the discrepancy between his transference expectations and the reality sitting in front of him. This can be implemented sometimes very directly by asking the patient to describe physically the therapist or the group member involved in the transference, and by helping him see and experience in vivid concrete detail the discrepancies between transference fantasies and reality. In doing this, we are asking him simply *to come to his senses;* to cut for a moment through the filtering fog of fantasy which he maintains around himself and experience the reality of the person who sits across from him. Simple as it sounds, when this is done at the actual moment of distorted perception, it can be effective in jarring the patient into closer touch with the real world of his own senses.

References

Berne, E. *Transactional analysis in psychotherapy.* New York: Grove, 1961.

Kempler, W. Experiential family therapy. *International Journal of Group Psychotherapy,* 1965, *15,* 57–71.

Perls, F. S. *Ego, hunger and aggression.* London: Unwin, 1947.

Perls, F. S., Hefferline, R. F., & Goodman, P. *Gestalt therapy: Excitement and growth in the human personality.* New York: Julian Press, 1951. (Republished: Dell, 1965.)

Tomkins, S. *Affect, imagery, consciousness.* Vol. 2. New York: Springer, 1963.

chapter 3

ONE GESTALT THERAPIST'S APPROACH*

Laura Perls

(At the Fourth Annual Conference of the American Academy of Psychotherapists in New York in 1959, leading therapists of five different orientations were asked a series of questions about their theoretical views and therapeutic approaches. Representing Gestalt therapy, Dr. Laura Perls gave the following answers.)

What do you do with the reluctant patient—either poorly referred or poorly motivated?

All patients are reluctant about something or other, sometime or other. Almost all patients are poorly motivated in the sense that they come, or are made to come, for the wrong reasons. I am suspicious of the patient who shows a great deal of insight and wears his suffering on the tip of his tongue. And I am wary of the overeager, enthusiastically cooperative patient who agrees and confirms, picks up the jargon in a

* Adapted by permission of the author and publisher from *Annals of Psychotherapy*, Special Combined Issue edited by J. Barron & R. A. Harper, Vols. 1 and 2, 1961.

jiffy, and dreams to order. He is reluctant to experience and express his differences of opinion, his doubts and objections.

But altogether, I am not particularly interested in the questions of motivation and referral. I take the patient as he presents himself at the time of his session with me. He was motivated enough to come for that appointment, and we take it from there, making contact with one another strictly on the basis of our mutual awareness at the time. Focusing on *what is* rather than on *what is not* or *what should be* usually gives the patient sufficient support to come for the next session—not necessarily better motivation for "having therapy" but at least a willingness to continue contact with the therapist.

Have you ever made a home call, and why?

I have made home calls only in cases of immobilizing accidents and in two cases of agoraphobia. After a few weeks both of the latter patients were able to come to my office.

How do you deal with a patient's reluctance to pay for things?

The patient who forgets or refuses to pay the therapist's fees will give indications of his reluctance right from the beginning in respect not only to money but to anything else you may ask of him: punctuality for appointments, information, expression of opinions and feelings, attempting an experiment, evaluation of his own or other peoples' attitudes and actions. He may be reluctant for many reasons: fear or spite, a confused sense of values, an infantile need to be cared for without having to do anything in return.

These are the problems that ultimately must be tackled.

In the meantime, of course, he can be coaxed and prodded into paying reluctantly, one way or another. You must make it clear that whatever you do for or with him cannot be evaluated and compensated for in money. What he pays for is your time and your attention. Everything that takes place during the session is in the services of his needs, even those demands we make of him that at the time make him anxious or uncomfortable. For his own needs the therapist asks only the regular payment. This explanation is usually intellectually accepted as fair, but you will find that the patient's reluctance changes into genuine willingness to pay only when he has developed an awareness of his own value. Only he who *has* and *is* can *give*.

On the other hand, the regularly paying patient is not necessarily the most genuinely promising one. He may get some secret satisfaction from his family's sacrifices for him or he may be buying you off.

There is also the window-shopping patient who precisely does *not* "buy," but pays the admission fee for a consultation as for a fashion show, tries out the analyst for size, and repeats the same stunt with another therapist during the next "season" of confusion or depression. I find that my awareness of the patient's "style," and the fact that I show him only what immediately "fits" him, usually makes him "buy." So I get stuck finally with the window-shopper, saddled not only with his "reluctance" but also with the particular problems accruing from his former abortive attempts at therapy. But this is another story!

Do you assume that you unconsciously want every one of your patients to get better?

This is a question that I cannot answer—I don't know what I unconsciously want. As far as I am aware, I want my patients to get better. If they don't, then I have to search for what I have failed to become aware of or to make them aware of in the ongoing relationship.

Do you assume that all your awareness and feelings, if shared with the patient, have therapeutic value?

I share *verbally* only as much of my awareness as will enable the patient to take the next step on his own, and lend him support for taking a risk in the context of his actual present malfunction. If I communicate too much, I may provoke a negative therapeutic reaction: intolerable anxiety, flight, resistance, paralysis, desensitization, projection. Of course, the patient learns to become aware of my reactions and expressions even if they are not verbalized.

Do you express your own problems or history at any time?

I will describe some problems and experiences from my own life or from other patients if I expect this to give support to the particular patient for a fuller realization of his own position and potentialities. In other words, only if it may help him to take the next step.

How do you control the acting-out patient?

This question seems to me to *create* a problem rather than to pinpoint one. Every patient, all the time, is acting in some way, and we call it "acting out" mainly when it is obviously undesirable, inadequate, exaggerated, overaggressive, perverted—that is, when it interrupts the patient's ongoing development and relationships. But the patient is or may be "acting out" when he behaves very correctly and even when he verbalizes most rationally and articulately. He will continue to "act out" as long as he has insufficient support for more appropriate behavior. So the task of therapy is not to interfere in or prevent his "acting out," which is at the time the only possible way for him to act, but to help him build up more adequate self-support for more continuously integrating and integrated behavior.

This time-consuming process is usually not aided by the imposition of restrictions, limitations, or threats, at least not as far as the patient's behavior outside the therapy situation is concerned. Within the therapy situation, some restrictions can be part of an experimental exploration of the patient's behavioral patterns and possibilities; but it is the *patient's* reaction that sets the limitations of tolerance of *therapist* behavior.

I am not punitive. I don't think that the attitude: "You better do what I am telling you, or else . . . !" goes with a genuine respect for the patient, whose resistances are his main support. To punish him for what he relies on most always provokes a negative reaction: fear, spite, resentment, vindictiveness, all of which interrupt the ongoing process of communication and understanding. The punitive therapist is himself "acting out" in the worst possible way; and he does so for the same reason as the "acting out" patient: because he does not know what else to do—because he himself has not enough support to give support where it is most needed.

What psychotherapeutic physical contact do you engage in with male or female patients, and is there a difference?

This question of *physical contact with the patient*

I shall answer very briefly. I will use any sort of physical contact if I expect it to facilitate the patient's next step in his awareness of the actual situation and what he is doing (or not doing) in and with it. I have no special rules with regard to male or female patients. I will light a cigarette, feed someone with a spoon, fix a girl's hair, hold hands or hold a patient on my lap—if that appears to be the best means of establishing the nonexistent or interrupted communication. I also touch patients or let them touch me in experiments to increase body-awareness: to point out tensions, malcoordination, rhythm of breathing, jerkiness, or fluidity in motion, etc.

There seems to be great divergence of opinion and a lot of anxiety about the admissibility of physical contact in therapy. If we want to help our patients to realize themselves more fully as truly *human* beings, we ourselves must have the courage to risk the dangers of being human.

What does your school say about the basic nature of man, and how does it affect your treatment process?

I am sorry that this has been put as the last question, for I consider it the most important one, in the light of which all the others either make sense or are irrelevant. I believe that not only every therapeutic measure, but every single thought and act is informed by our basic conviction of what makes man "human," even if we never manifestly express this conviction and take it so much for granted that we are hardly aware of it ourselves. Speaking strictly for myself—the only way a Gestalt therapist can say anything at all—I am deeply convinced that the basic problem not only of therapy but of life is *how to make life livable for a being whose dominant characteristic is his awareness of himself as a unique individual on the one hand and of his mortality on the other.* The first gives him a feeling of overwhelming importance and the other a feeling of fear and frustration. Suspended between these poles, he vibrates in a state of inevitable tension and anxiety that, at least to modern Western man, seems unrelievable. This causes various neurotic solutions that are prevalent not only in our patients but to a greater or lesser degree in our total culture.

When awareness and the expression of uniqueness and individuality are repressed, we have uniformity, boredom, and ultimate meaninglessness of mass culture, in which the awareness of one's own dying becomes so intolerable that it has to be alienated at any price, by "having fun" with accumulated inanities or artificial excitements (alcohol, dope, delinquency). When uniqueness and individuality are overemphasized, we have a false "humanism" with man as the measure of all things, resulting in exaggerated expectations, frustration, and disappointment. As a reaction-formation, we find either a false detachment, a hopeless or blasé laissez faire, or a false commitment, a frantic pursuit of a pseudocreativeness (the obsessional fiddling around with "hobbies" and "cultural activities," from do-it-yourself painting of the kitchen shelves to "seeing my analyst" or going to church).

Real creativeness, in my experience, is inextricably linked with the awareness of mortality. The sharper this awareness, the greater the urge to bring forth something new, to participate in the infinitely continuing creativeness in nature. This is what makes out of sex, love; out of the herd, society; out of wheat and fruit, bread and wine; and out of sound, music. This is what makes life livable and—incidentally—makes therapy possible.

As long as the Judaeo-Christian orientation was the structural mainstay of his society and personality, Western man could accept the identity of living and dying without questioning. In the East, the aim of Zen Buddhism is precisely this realization of identity of living and dying, of commitment and detachment. In our Western world, the neurotic is the man who cannot face his own dying and therefore cannot live fully as a human being. Gestalt therapy, with its emphasis on immediate awareness and involvement, offers a method for developing the necessary support for a self-continuing creative adjustment—which is the only way of coping with the experience of dying and, therefore, of living.

chapter 4

THERAPY IN GROUPS: PSYCHOANALYTIC, EXPERIENTIAL, AND GESTALT

Ruth C. Cohn

Within the past twenty years group therapy has found ever-enlarging circles of application, accelerated by the needs of large groups (military, educational, civic, and business), the desire to reduce the length and cost of treatment for the mentally ill, and the search by many individuals for a less painful and more meaningful existence. During this period psychotherapists have acquired more experience, knowledge, and skill, which has led to modifications of individual psychotherapy and new models of group therapy.

This paper will describe three models of group therapy. It does not claim scholarly precision; rather, it is based on my personal impressions and theoretical reflections about the three models of group therapy I have experienced as a participant and practiced as a coleader with pioneering group therapists in analytic, experiential, and Gestalt methods. Among those practitioners were the group analysts Alexander Wolf, Asya Kadis, the late Sandy Flowermann, and Hyman

Spotnitz; the experiential therapists Carl Whitaker, John Warkentin, and many close friends in the American Academy of Psychotherapists; and Frederick Perls as a teacher in Gestalt therapy workshops.*

Psychoanalytic Therapy in Groups

The therapist creates a setting in which verbal exploration and interaction are facilitated. The interaction among group members helps the individual explore his behavior patterns, feelings, and thoughts, and helps him understand his historical and present psychodynamics. The group analyst's goal is to stimulate interaction, differentiate content in the group, and communicate interpretation of meanings of personal and interpersonal threads.

Psychoanalytic theory regards a person as sick as long as he is unable to perceive and make choices realistically. His ego—the central function of perceiving, integrating, and executing—is not sufficiently in charge. He is misled by faulty perceptual, emotional, and cognitive fixations stemming from distortions established in early childhood. These distortions have various causes, such as undeveloped abilities (spotty ego-development), infantile misperceptions, or identification with neurotic or psychotic adults. The persistence of such distortions is mainly due to their being rooted in early childhood. Such distortions are often not suspected by the neurotic who believes that his world image is realistic until he fails badly and repeatedly because of his illusion. (A person who has always worn purple glasses could hardly avoid perceiving a

* James Simkin, from whom I have learned a great deal about Gestalt therapy, was not using group therapy at that time.

purple world; a more accurate perception could occur only if he were to remove the glasses and be confronted with his error.)

Analytic therapy aims at improving perception and reality adjustment. The neurotic may wish for such change, yet resistance to basic changes is as much a biological factor as is the drive for improvement and growth. The patient's resistances to recognizing reality are fortified by the (unconscious) wish to hold onto his early defenses, which have protected him from his archaic fears of isolation, mutilation, and destruction. While children establish pseudosecurity in their illusionary world (by such fantasies as imagining their parents to be omnipotent and to own magic powers), they simultaneously create a future set of transferences into which each newcomer in life can be fitted. The patient either fits people into his transference images or chooses partners (mates, friends, bosses, etc.) who are likely to play the assigned transference roles that, as a child, he attributed to the important figures in his limited universe.

In the therapeutic process the psychoanalyst must take into account the patient's defenses against any change threatening the foundation of his pseudosecurity. He will give up his defenses of helplessness and omnipotence only when he experiences his realistic potency evolving from greater ego-integration of liberated id and superego forces. The recovering patient learns to accept the realistic insecurity inherent in the lot of man.

Group therapy is a new analytic tool with the same aim. Whereas in individual analysis the patient meets with only one other person onto whom he transfers the various relationship patterns of his childhood, in the therapy group he has several people to endow with these qualities. A network of multiple transferences ensues. Also, in individual analysis the therapist uses skilled efforts not to reveal his personality traits and feelings unless they are directly induced by the patient, but in group analysis he has moved his chair from behind the couch into the circle of his patients. With this gesture he has lost his traditional invisibility but not his value as a transference object. Furthermore, the patient meets head-on the open reality of his peers. To the surprise of the analytic profession, the transference buds, which previously had been protected and nurtured (to bring them to full bloom before they would be analyzed), proved to be much hardier than had been suspected: transferences, remained all-pervasive even in full view of the peer group's nonneutral, nonmirrorlike behavior.

The group analyst stimulates interaction with questions, silence, comments, and interpretations; he accepts expressions of the here-and-now events in the group as well as communications about the there and then of the patient's life.

He encourages group members to tell their dreams and fantasies and to relate their associations and feelings to each other. He may concentrate on one person at a time and use the group as assistant therapists, or he may address most of his interventions to the group as a whole. For instance, the interaction of one "monopolizing" member in a group could be approached in three analytically correct ways: (1) "Why does X talk so much? What does he want or fear to express?" (2) "Why is the group so silent? What does the group achieve, avoid, or use X for?" (3) X speaks: all others are silent." (Description.)

Psychoanalytic group therapy relies on verbalization as the only acceptable vehicle of communication and integration. All nonverbal expressions are regarded as "acting in" (when it occurs during the session) and "acting out" when the patient symbolizes his conflict in activity outside the group. Both are analyzed as resistance against analytic insight; for example, the patient may resent the analyst or a group member, yet instead of searching for the childhood facsimile of this resentment, he acts out against his boss and thereby keeps his transference world intact. He has shed the resentful emotion without therapeutic gain.

No physical touching is allowed in the session, and personal motor expressions are permitted only as small expressive gesticulations. Kicking or walking around would be interpreted as resistance against insight and integration. Some analysts even forbid smoking or drinking coffee in order to maintain a high level of frustration, which they believe to be the necessary driving force for inducing change. Most analytic group therapists forbid social contact of their group patients, although "alternate sessions" (therapeutic sessions without the analyst) are supported by many. Such alternate sessions provide a specific forum for the special family transference pattern: the feeling of children in the absence of their parents.

Cure in analysis is seen as the process by which disassociated parts of the patient's perceptual, emotional, and cognitive world are integrated. In group analysis this process is supported and furthered by various "corrective emotional experiences" among the patients and between the patients and therapist. Analysis does not promote any specific value in living other than that of free choice versus fixated unconscious bondage. As each patient reveals himself in verbalizing his past and present life story and conflicts, he also reenacts and reexperiences past feelings in the pseudo-family constellation of his therapy group.

The process of sorting out what has irrationally been carried over from the past into the present takes place through emotional and cognitive confrontation, analysis, and interpretation of what *is* rather than what has been fancied. Under the guidance of an unrevealing but accepting therapist, the triad of the curative process takes place: (1) the analysis and lowering of archaic defensiveness, (2) the experience and interpretation of transference illusions, and (3) the corrective emotional experience within a self-revealing group of fellow patients.

Experiential Therapy in Groups

Like his analytic colleague, the experiential therapist creates an atmosphere in which free communications and interaction are promoted. However, his primary interests are immediate behavior and feelings rather than psychodynamic connections and interpretations. He is concerned with the *how* of the patient's dealings within his family, his job situation, and the present group setting rather than with the *why*. The guiding concepts are not transference and resistance, but authenticity and directness. His main tool is exposing himself as an authentic and direct human being, and he affirms his unique identity in stead confrontation with the group.

The group members are encouraged to state whatever they feel and think. The therapeutic goal is the acceptance of being in the fluidity of life with its pleasures and pains, and in the ambiguity of existence in the face of death. The way is the goal, the "courage to be" and the honesty of communications. While the group analyst stimulates interaction by imposing the frustration of his relative silence and withholding of private communications, the experiential group therapist enters the group process as a partner. For him the group session is not a laboratory in which old family patterns are relived, explored, and replaced with a better set of relationships, but an important part of living that differs from other situations only by its greater authenticity, directness, and concentration on the essence of living. (An experientialist, whose name I don't recall, said that the end of formal therapy can be defined as the point in time when the patient is able to use any life situation as therapeutic.)

The experientialist, of course, does not indiscriminately act upon his feelings or reveal everything and anything to the group. The experientialist is not impulsive but states himself in the interest of the therapeutic process. He chooses from the multitude of his experiences those events, feelings, and thoughts that he judges or intuits to be relevant to the specific situation. I have labeled his choice of self-statements "selective authenticity." Such statements must feel right to him, must be in tune with his patient's needs and his own needs. His personal communications, however, are not limited by their content; they may include embarrassing and painful events as well as happy and proud experiences, or dreams and fantasies.

In experiential group therapy, words, although prevalent, are not the only form of interactional communication. All honest self-statements are permitted and cherished. These may include physical signs of affection and rejection (punching bags or throw pillows may be used). Excluded are sexual intercourse and damage to furnishings and people.

The experientialist, like the psychoanalyst, avoids social mingling with his patients although, generally speaking, he is less likely to request his patients to refrain from meeting socially. (Mingling with patients outside the therapy sessions became an overwhelming burden to most experientialists who tried this "more natural" structure in earlier years; difficulties in maintaining the necessary therapeutic honesty were greater than they could comfortably manage.)

Although there are different modalities of working as an analytic group therapist (determined by the therapist's personality and his various viewpoints of group analysis), the analytic group therapy model is more clearly defined than the experiential one. It is more likely that the student analyst would be told by his "control" analyst that he was right or wrong, correct or incorrect in his therapeutic work than that the student of the experiential school would be so evaluated by his supervisor. In an analytic group there are more factual data to be accounted for (establishing case histories, psychodynamic connections, exploration of transference and countertransference patterns and defense mechanisms) than there are in the experiential setting, where the therapeutic emphasis is placed on the individual's uniqueness and spontaneity in group interaction. The quality of experiential therapy depends on the therapist's mature and broad approach to life. He also needs knowledge of psychodynamics, trained intuition, and many interactional techniques (such as role-playing, encounter games, sensitivity training, etc.), but basically, the more he is in touch with himself and the world, the fuller is the reservoir of offerings with which he can intuitively and creatively react to his patients.

Gestalt Therapy in Groups

At this point, I feel drawn to a more subjective form of writing. Frederick Perls has in the past few years created a workshop model which represents a new way of using a group in psychotherapy. I will therefore present the Gestalt therapy model by discussing my experience with Perls.* The primary difference in Perls's approach is his making group interaction almost taboo. "Who wants to work with me now? I am available" is the extended invitation. The patient is always a volunteer with whom Perls will work for ten or a hundred minutes, as the situation requires, with the group mainly observing. In my opinion, Perls is a radical experientialist in his request for the *now* of experiencing. I also see him as an "instant detective" skilled in drawing a vertical line through the mud of details and the rocks of defenses straight to the core of the patient's emotional fixations, which he calls "unfinished business." Perls asks the patient for his *now*, which means to stay in the "stream of awareness" and "to lose his mind and find his senses." He stays with the patient in close perceptual contact, usually close enough to touch, often asking the patient what he sees or hears, rather than what he thinks.

Perls's attentiveness is to the obvious and subtle

* Many of his followers are using a combination of interactional techniques with Perls's workshop model. Among those I know are John Brinley, Joen Fagan, Erving Polster, Irma Shepherd, and myself.

discrepancies in physical and verbal expressions, such as the sound of the voice giving a different message than the spoken words. An inappropriate smile or "canceling" manual gesture may express what the patient does not dare to think or hides behind flat "preachings." Perls also challenges the patient to engage in a role-playing dialogue between discrepant facets of his personality, or he will ask the patient to tell a dream and thereafter to let each part of the dream talk for itself (like objects in a fairy tale). The patient acts out every detail of the dream, be it a person, a chair, a body part, a house, or a country. It (he) talks. This resembles fiction-writing in reverse. The invented fictional parts talk to their author (dreamer), who had not been aware of inventing them. The patient now listens to his self-invented creatures, who rise from the status of rejected or unknown procreations to emotionally exciting and accepted parts of the personal self.

Perls, like Freud, treats the dream as the royal road to discovery and progress. However, his technique for using dreams is experiential rather than analytic. The patient experiences the explicitly verbal and play-acted statements of his dream parts and listens to their messages. Free associations, spiraling around the core of meaning toward the essence of the dream, are replaced by dream voices that form an orchestrated chorus. The music evolves in the process of singing and does not require interpretation. The "medium is the message."

The similarity and contrast of psychoanalysis and Gestalt therapy are most clearly evidenced in their regard for dreams. The analyst invites an abundance of images and thoughts into the dreamer's awareness, helping him to integrate split-off events and feelings of his past and present life. In group analysis, this endeavor is supported by multiple transference projections onto the group members. Their reactions, associations, and interpretations help the patient (through the similarity of unconscious processes) to widen and deepen his understanding of the dream. (The Jungian concept of the "collective unconscious" helps clarify this process.)

The Gestalt therapist relates to the immediacy of the dreams' statements by moving in and focusing spotlights on each segment. This procedure connects emotional present and past into a telescopic multi-exposure and leads towards the relevant "unfinished business."

Avoidance and *unfinished business* are, in my opinion, Perls's core concepts in Gestalt therapy. Unfinished business includes emotions, events, memories, which linger unexpressed in the organismic person; avoidance is the means by which one keeps away from the unfinished business. By avoidance the person tries to escape from feelings that must be felt in order to release him into his own custody.

These concepts and hypotheses certainly sound familiar to the psychoanalyst and appear to be almost identical with the concepts of integrating repressed unconscious material under the supremacy of the ego as guiding power. However, although the concepts of avoidance and unfinished business are closely related to the analytic concepts of resistance and fixation, the differences in wording signal essential differences between the two approaches. "Resistance and fixation express the deterministic philosophy of cause-and-effect-oriented thinking; the analyst "treats" the patient and "controls" the student. He takes responsibility for his interventions as carefully as the contractor plans his work with the demolition crew, the architect, and the builders. Avoidance and unfinished business belong to a philosophy that challenges the patient to take responsibility for whatever he is. The therapist or teacher helps him own up to himself by stimulating responses to areas of his blindness.

Correspondingly, Perls does not appear to be a therapist in the analytic or experiential sense of the word, but rather a Zen master who guides his apprentice on the paradoxic road to self-mastery, discipline, and freedom. He teaches the patient to do what he wants with every moment of his life rather than hiding behind "I can't" (which Perls patiently replaces over and over again with "Say: 'I don't want to' "), or behind "catastrophic expectations"—the fear of what will happen if he accepts whatever he really is and feels.

Unfinished business connotes the steadily nagging underground feelings that are not available to the patient in his daily living as long as he avoids confronting and fully experiencing his pain, anxiety, mourning, rage, etc. While the psychoanalyst times his interventions carefully, in order to reduce anxieties to a bearable level, Perls encourages the experience of the most intense emotions in the now of the therapeutic session. It is the catastrophic expectation of painful emotions and their psychophysical impact that magnifies anxiety, pain, and rage, and lets them linger on with their eroding and destructive power. Complete and unabashed acceptance of, and total abandonment to, feelings lead to "organismic change," which is an experience rather than an insight.*

Perls forbids *ifs*, *buts*, *I can'ts*, and *I feel guiltys* in the therapy session. *If* and *but* are replaced by *and; can't* by *I don't want to;* and *I feel guilty* by *I resent.* "I want to write to my friend but I can't" is translated into "I want to write to my friend and I don't want to write to him." The two confused wants are then unfused and talk for themselves or to each other, stating the emotional conflict in repeated and increasingly emotional forms, often taking on the pattern of the top-dog talking as the *should* ("You should write this letter") to the under-dog ("I don't want to write this letter"). As long as the pseudo conflict is repetitively reenacted, the under-dog always wins. (He makes sure that the letter is not being written. Guilt is the price the under-dog pays to the top-dog for winning—or the person to the friend for not writing.

The skillful separation of conflicts into their duality and their subsequent reenactment leads, after a series of dialogues, to feelings of blankness, confusion, helplessness, etc. This experience is the *impasse:* the ultimate expression of two strivings pulling in opposite directions. The therapist's guiding words are: "be blank," "be confused," "be empty." When the patient can endure and experience the extent of his feelings of confusion, blankness, impotence, etc., organismic change takes place. It is the theory of this impasse phenomenon which I regard as Perls's unique and most important contribution to psychotherapeutic practice. It has helped to improve the efficacy of psy-

* Insight, however, in my experience, usually follows sometime later, as in any other form of therapy—a fact I call the "cementing" function of interpretation.

chotherapy, both in depth and in speed, in an exhilarating and fruitful way.

Like most experientialists, Perls keeps the controls of "selective authenticity." However, he rarely communicates feelings that do not seem to be responses to the patient's behavior. This choice of communications resembles the analyst's maxim to express feelings only if and when they seem to be "induced" by the patient's behavior.

While Perls works with a volunteer patient in the group (nobody is ever requested or told to take the "hot seat"), the group must remain silent. However, at some point Perls brings the group into play in a unique way which I call the "Greek chorus method." The "Greek chorus" forecasts, underlines, and cements strivings and achievements of the working patient in a way that combines conditioning with a very limited but effective form of group interaction. For example, the patient has come to a therapeutic realization: "I don't have to live up to anybody's expectations." He is now asked to "make the rounds" and say to each participant this sentence, adding individual formulations such as "I am not here to live up to your expectations. I do not have to give you my chair when I don't want to," "I don't have to write a paper with you." The group members reply briefly with whatever their reactions are, such as, "You are right, you don't have to: Neither do I have to live up to yours," etc. Expressions of physical affections or rejection are permitted.

I have taught workshops on "Five Models of Group Interaction," which have included the experiential, analytic, and Gestalt therapy models together with the T-group and my own theme-centered interactional approach. In these workshops the students were led to experience each demonstrated model by participation. Invariably, the groups reacted with the greatest personal involvement in the Gestalt therapy workshop, in spite of the fact that they were spectators rather than interacting participants most of the time. Observing the dramatic therapeutic dialogue was of greater impact than personal interactional exchange. The patient's vertical plunge into previously avoided emotions seemed to touch the group of observers in the truest sense of identification and purification of a Greek drama. The members of the Greek chorus seem indeed to experience the tragic and joyful feelings of the patient's responses within themselves.*

In concluding, I want to describe an episode from one of Perls's workshops. He said, "Can you imagine that I, the Gestalt man, was ever a training analyst at an analytic institute?" And before I caught on to what I was saying, it popped out of my mouth, "That's why you are so good at it, Fritz." Since the phrase "*it* popped out of my mouth" is sacrilege for a Perls's student who is charged with owning her feelings and actions "per *I*" and not "per *it*," I will corroborate this statement with my credo. I am firmly convinced that Perls's skill in guiding patients to their unfinished business in a straight vertical line without overstepping their level of endurance is bound up with his rich back-

* However, in Gestalt therapy groups I have led, I became impressed with the participants' desire to work through the impact of the intense experiences they had had as observers. Therefore I either have combined the Gestalt workshop with post-sessions of interaction, or have used group-integrating techniques within the Gestalt therapy dialogue. The group has also occasionally taken over the role of the therapist.

ground knowledge and experience. These include theory and practice of psychoanalytic therapy, the acceptance of the experiential credo of the here-and-now values of authenticity and directness, acquaintance with Moreno's psychodrama and with Zen philosophy, and work with body awareness. In the same historical sequence, the three models of group therapy presented in this paper have developed from earlier procedures and each has, in important aspects, superseded what has gone before.

chapter 5

THE RULES AND GAMES OF GESTALT THERAPY

Abraham Levitsky and Frederick S. Perls

The techniques of Gestalt therapy revolve largely around two sets of guidelines which we will call "rules" and "games." The rules are few in number and are usually introduced and described formally at the outset. The games, on the other hand, are numerous and no definitive list is possible since an ingenious therapist may well devise new ones from time to time.

If we are to do justice at all to the spirit and essence of Gestalt therapy, we must recognize clearly the distinction between rules and commandments. The philosophy of rules is to provide us with effective means of unifying thought with feeling. They are designed to help us dig out resistances, promote heightened awareness—to facilitate the maturation process. They are definitely *not* intended as a dogmatic list of *do*'s and *don'ts*; rather, they are offered in the spirit of experiments that the patient may perform. They will often provide considerable shock value and thus demonstrate to the patient the many and subtle ways in which he prevents himself from fully experiencing himself and his environment.

When the intention of the rules is truly appreciated,

they will be understood in their inner meaning and not in their literal sense. The "good boy" for instance, totally incapable of understanding the liberating intent of the rules, will frequently follow them exactly but to absurdity, thus endowing them with his own bloodlessness rather than with the vitality they seek to promote.

True to its heritage in Gestalt psychology, the essence of Gestalt therapy is in the perspective with which it views human life processes. Seen in this light, any particular set of techniques such as our presently used rules and games will be regarded merely as convenient means—useful tools for our purposes but without sacrosanct qualities.

THE RULES

The principle of the now. The idea of the now, of the immediate moment, of the content and structure of present experience is one of the most potent, most pregnant, and most elusive principles of Gestalt therapy. Speaking from my own experience [A.L.], I have been at various times intrigued, angered, baffled, and exhilarated by the implications of the seemingly simple idea "being in the now." And what a fascinating experience it is to help others become aware of the manifold ways in which they prevent themselves from having true immediate awareness.

In order to promote *now* awareness, we encourage communications in the present tense. "What is your present awareness?" "What is happening now?" "What do you feel at this moment?" The phrase "What is your *now?*" is an effective one from therapist to patient.

It would not be accurate to say that there is no interest in historical material and in the past. This material is dealt with actively when it is felt to be germane to important themes of the present personality structure. However, the most effective means of integrating past material into the personality is to bring it—as fully as possible—into the present. In this way we avoid the bland, intellectualized "aboutisms" and strive vigorously to give all material the impact of immediacy. When the patient refers to events of yesterday, last week, or last year, we quickly direct him to "be there" in fantasy and to enact the drama in present terms.

We are active in pointing out to the patient how easily he leaves the now. We identify his need to bring into the dialogue absent individuals, the nostalgic urge to reminisce, the tendency to get preoccupied with fears and fantasies of the future. For most of us, the exercise of remaining in present awareness is a taxing discipline that can be maintained only for short periods. It is a discipline to which we are not accustomed and which we are inclined to resist.

I and thou. With this principle, we strive to drive home as concretely as possible the notion that true communication involves both sender and receiver. The patient often behaves as if his words are aimed at the blank wall or at thin air. When he is asked, "To whom are you saying this?" he is made to face his reluctance to send his message directly and unequivocally to the receiver, to the *other*.

Thus the patient is often directed to invoke the other's name—if necessary, at the beginning of each sentence. He is asked to be aware of the distinction between "talking to" and "talking at" the listener. He is led to discover whether his voice and words are truly reaching the other. Is he really touching the other with his words? How far is he willing to touch the other with his words? Can he begin to see that this phobic avoidance of relating to others, of making genuine contact with others is also manifested in his voice mechanisms and his verbal behavior? If he has slight or insufficient contact, can he begin to realize his serious doubts as to whether others actually exist for him in this world; as to whether he is truly *with* people or feeling alone and abandoned?

"It" language and "I" language. This rule deals with the semantics of responsibility and involvement. It is common for us to refer to our bodies and to our acts and behaviors in distantiated, third person, *it* language:

> What do you feel in your eye?
> *It is blinking.*
>
> What is your hand doing?
> *It is trembling.*
>
> What do you experience in your throat?
> *It is choked.*
>
> What do you hear in your voice?
> *It is sobbing.*

Through the simple—and seemingly mechanical—expedient of changing *it* language into *I* language we learn to identify more closely with the particular behavior in question and to assume responsibility for it.

Instead of "It is trembling," "*I* am trembling." Rather than "It is choked," "*I* am choked." Going one step further, rather than "I am choked," "I am choking myself." Here we can immediately see the different degree of responsibility and involvement that is experienced.

Changing *it* to *I* is an example in microcosm of many of the Gestalt game techniques. As the patient participates, he is far more likely to see himself as an active agent who does things rather than a passive creature to whom things somehow "happen."

A number of other semantic games are available. If the patient says, "I can't do that," the therapist will ask, "Can you say, I *won't* do that?" As the patient accepts and uses this formulation, the therapist will follow with "And what do you experience now?"

> T.: What do you hear in your voice?
> P.: My voice sounds like it is crying.
> T.: Can you take responsibility for that by saying, "I am crying"?

Other gambits in the semantics of responsibility are having the patient substitute verbs for nouns and frequently use the imperative mode of speech as the most direct means of communication.

Use of the awareness continuum. The use of the so-called awareness continuum—the "*how*" of experience—is absolutely basic to Gestalt therapy. With it we often achieve effects both striking and startling. The frequent return to and reliance on the awareness continuum is one of the major innovations in technique contributed by Gestalt therapy. The method is quite simple:

> T.: What are you aware of now?
> P.: Now I am aware of talking to you. I see others in the room. I'm aware of John squirming. I can

feel the tension in my shoulders. I'm aware that I get anxious as I say this.

T.: How do you experience the anxiety?

P.: I hear my voice quiver. My mouth feels dry. I talk in a very halting way.

T.: Are you aware of what your eyes are doing?

P.: Well, now I realize that my eyes keep looking away—

T.: Can you take responsibility for that?

P.: —that I keep looking away from you.

T.: Can you be your eyes now? Write the dialogue for them.

P.: I am Mary's eyes. I find it hard to gaze steadily. I keep jumping and darting about. . . .

The awareness continuum has inexhaustible applications. Primarily, however, it is an effective way of guiding the individual to the firm bedrock of his experiences and away from the endless verbalizations, explanations, interpretations. Awareness of body feelings and of sensations and perceptions constitutes our most certain—perhaps our only certain—knowledge. Relying on information provided in awareness is the best method of implementing Perls's dictum to "lose your mind and come to your senses."

The use of the awareness continuum is the Gestalt therapist's best means of leading the patient away from the emphasis on the *why* of behavior (psychoanalytic interpretation) and toward the *what* and the *how* of behavior (experiential psychotherapy):

P.: I feel afraid.

T.: How do you experience the fear?

P.: I can't see you clearly. My hands are perspiring. . . .

As we help the patient rely on his senses ("return to his senses"), we also help him distinguish between the reality *out there* and the frightening goblins he manufactures in his own fantasies:

P.: I'm sure people will despise me for what I just said.
T.: Go around the room and look at us carefully. Tell me what you *see*, what your eyes—not your imaginings—tell you.
P.: (*after some moments of exploration and discovery*) Well, actually people don't *look* so rejecting! Some of you even look warm and friendly!
T.: What do you experience now?
P.: I'm more relaxed now.

No gossiping. As is the case with many Gestalt techniques, the no-gossiping rule is designed to promote feelings and to prevent avoidance of feelings. Gossiping is defined as talking about an individual when he is actually present and could just as well be addressed directly. For example, let us say the therapist is dealing with Bill and Ann:

P.: (*to therapist*) The trouble with Ann is she's always picking on me.
T.: You're gossiping; say this to Ann.
P.: (*turning to Ann*) You're always picking on me.

We often gossip about people when we have not been able to handle directly the feelings they arouse in us. The no-gossiping rule is another Gestalt technique that facilitates direct confrontation of feelings.

Asking questions. Gestalt therapy gives a good deal of attention to the patient's need to ask questions. The questioner is obviously saying, "Give me, tell me . . ." Careful listening will often reveal that the questioner does not really need information, or that the question is not really necessary, or that it represents laziness and passivity on the part of the patient. The therapist may then say, "Change that question into a statement." The frequency with which the patient can actually do this validates the action of the therapist.

Genuine questions are to be distinguished from hypocritical questions. The latter are intended to manipulate or cajole the other into seeing or doing things a particular way. On the other hand, questions in the form of "How are you doing?" and "Are you aware that . . ." provide genuine support.

The Games

Following is a brief description of a number of "games" used in Gestalt therapy. They are proposed by the therapist when the moment—in terms of either the individual's or the group's needs—seems appropriate. Some of the games, such as the "I have a secret" game or the "I take responsibility" game are particularly useful as group warm-ups at the beginning of a session.

It is, of course, no accident that some of the major techniques of Gestalt therapy are couched in game form. This is evidently a basic metacommunication on the part of Perls, highlighting one of the many facets of his philosophy of personality functioning. The game language (itself a game) can be seen as a commentary on the nature of all or most of social behavior. The message is *not* to stop playing games, since every form of social organization can be seen as one or another game form. Rather the message is to be aware of the games we play and to be free to substitute satisfying for nonsatisfying games. Applying this view to any two-person relationship (love, marriage, friendship), we would not be inclined to seek out a partner who "does not play games" but rather one whose games fit comfortably with our own.

Games of dialogue. In trying to effect integrated functioning, the Gestalt therapist seeks out whatever divisions or splits are manifested in the personality. Naturally, whatever "split" is found is a function of the therapist's frame of reference and his observational powers. One of the main divisions postulated is that between the so-called top-dog and under-dog. Top-dog is roughly the equivalent of the psychoanalytic superego. Top-dog moralizes, specializes in *shoulds,* and is generally bossy and condemning. Under-dog tends to be passively resistant, makes excuses, and finds reasons to delay.

When this division is encountered, the patient is asked to have an actual dialogue between these two components of himself. The same game of dialogue can, of course, be pursued for any significant split within the personality (aggressive versus passive, "nice guy" versus scoundrel, masculine versus feminine, etc.). At times the dialogue game can even be applied with various body parts such as right hand versus left, or upper body versus lower. The dialogue can also be developed between the patient and some significant person. The patient simply addresses the person as if he were there, imagines the response, replies to the response, etc.

Making the rounds. The therapist may feel that a particular theme or feeling expressed by the patient should be faced vis-à-vis every other person in the group. The patient may have said, "I can't stand anyone in this room." The therapist will then say, "OK, make the rounds. Say that to each one of us, and add some other remark pertaining to your feelings about each person."

The "rounds" game is of course infinitely flexible and need not be confined to verbal interaction. It may involve touching, caressing, observing, frightening, etc.

Unfinished business. Unfinished business is the Gestalt therapy analogue of the perceptual or cognitive incomplete task of Gestalt psychology. Whenever unfinished business (unresolved feelings) is identified, the patient is asked to complete it. Obviously all of us have endless lists of unfinished business in the realm of interpersonal relations, with, for instance, parents, siblings, friends. Perls contends that resentments are the most common and important kinds of unfinished business.

"I take responsibility." In this game we build on some of the elements of the awareness continuum but we consider all perceptions to be acts. With each statement, we ask patients to use the phrase, ". . . and I take responsibility for it." For example, "I am aware that I move my leg . . . and I take responsibility for it." "My voice is very quiet . . . and I take responsibility for it." "Now I don't know what to say . . . and I take responsibility for not knowing."

What seems at first blush a mechanical, even foolish procedure is soon seen as one heavily laden with meaning.

"I have a secret." This game permits exploration of feelings of guilt and shame. Each person thinks of a

well-guarded personal secret. He is instructed *not* to share the secret itself but to imagine (project) how he feels others would react to it. A further step can then be for each person to boast about what a terrible secret he nurses. The unconscious attachment to the secret as a precious achievement now begins to come to light.

Playing the projection. Many seeming perceptions are projections. For instance, the patient who says, "I can't trust you," may be asked to play the role of an untrustworthy person in order to discover his own inner conflict in this area. Another patient may complain to the therapist, "You're not really interested in me. You just do this for a living." He will be told to enact this attitude, after which he might be asked whether this is possibly a trait he himself possesses.

Reversals. One way in which the Gestalt therapist approaches certain symptoms or difficulties is to help the patient realize that overt behavior commonly represents the reversal of underlying or latent impulses. We therefore use the reversal technique. For example, the patient claims to suffer from inhibition or excessive timidity. He will be asked to play an exhibitionist. In taking this plunge into an area fraught with anxiety, he makes contact with a part of himself that has long been submerged. Or, the patient may wish to work on his problem of extreme touchiness to criticism. He will be asked to play the role of listening very carefully to everything that is said to him—especially criticism—without the need to defend or counterattack. Or, the patient may be unassertive and overly sweet; he will be asked to play the part of an uncooperative and spiteful person.

The rhythm of contact and withdrawal. Following its interest in the totality of life processes, in the phenomena of figure and ground, Gestalt therapy emphasizes the polar nature of vital functioning. The capacity for love is impaired by the inability to sustain anger. Rest is needed to restore energy. A hand is neither open nor closed but capable of both functions.

The natural inclination toward withdrawal from contact, which the patient will experience from time to time, is not dealt with as a resistance to be overcome but as a rhythmic response to be respected. Consequently when the patient wishes to withdraw, he is asked to close his eyes and withdraw in fantasy to any place or situation in which he feels secure. He describes the scene and his feelings there. Soon he is asked to open his eyes and "come back to the group." The on-going work is then resumed, usually with new material provided by the patient who has now had some of his energies restored by his withdrawal.

The Gestalt approach suggests that we accept withdrawal needs in any situation where attention or interest has lagged but that we remain aware of where our attention goes.

"Rehearsal." According to Perls, a great deal of our thinking consists of internal rehearsal and preparation for playing our accustomed social roles. The experience of stage fright simply presents our fear that we will not conduct our roles well. The group therefore plays the game of sharing rehearsals with each other, thus becoming more aware of the preparatory means employed in bolstering our social roles.

"Exaggeration." This game is closely allied to the principle of the awareness continuum and provides us with another means of understanding body language.

There are many times when the patient's unwitting movement or gesture appears to be a significant communication. However, the gestures may be abortive, undeveloped or incomplete—perhaps a wave of the arm or a tap of the leg. The patient will be asked to exaggerate the movement repeatedly, usually making the inner meaning more apparent. Sometimes the patient will be asked to develop the movement into a dance to get more of his self into integrative expression.

A similar technique is used for purely verbal behavior and can well be called the "repetition" game. A patient may make a statement of importance but has perhaps glossed over it or in some way indicated that he has not fully absorbed its impact. He will be asked to say it again—if necessary a great number of times—and, where necessary, louder and louder. Soon he is really hearing himself and not just forming words.

"May I feed you a sentence?" In listening to or observing the patient, the therapist may conclude that a particular attitude or message is implied. He will then say, "May I feed you a sentence? Say it and try it on for size. Say it to several people here." He then proposes his sentence, and the patient tests out his reaction to the sentence. Typically, the therapist does not simply interpret for or to the patient. Although there is obviously a strong interpretative element here, the patient must make the experience his own through active participation. If the proposed sentence is truly a key sentence, spontaneous development of the idea will be supplied by the patient.

Marriage counseling games. We will mention only a few of the great number of possible variations on these games.

The partners face each other and take turns saying sentences beginning with, "I resent you for . . ." The resentment theme can then be followed by the appreciation theme, "What I appreciate in you is . . ." Then the spite theme, "I spite you by . . ." Or, the compliance theme, "I am compliant by . . ."

Lastly, there is the discovery theme. The partners alternate describing each other in sentences beginning with "I see . . . " Many times this process of discovery involves actually seeing each other for the first time. Since, as Perls points out, the most difficult problem in marriage is that of being in love with a concept rather than an individual, we must learn to distinguish between our fantasied image and the flesh-and-blood person.

Finally, we should mention a particular approach that does not fall under the heading of either rules or games but which can well be included at this point. It is an important gambit in Gestalt therapy and symbolizes much of Perls's underlying philosophy. We might call it the principle of "Can you stay with this feeling?" This technique is invoked at key moments when the patient refers to a feeling or mood or state of mind that is unpleasant and that he has a great urge to dispel. Let us say he has arrived at a point where he feels empty or confused or frustrated or discouraged. The therapist says, "Can you stay with this feeling?"

This is almost always a dramatic moment and a frustrating one for the patient. He has referred to his experience with some sourness and an obviously impatient desire to get on with it, to leave this feeling well behind him. The therapist however asks him deliberately to remain with whatever psychic pain he has at the moment. The patient will be asked to elaborate the *what* and *how* of his feelings. "What are your sensations?" "What are your perceptions, fantasies, expectancies?" At these moments, it is frequently most appropriate and necessary to help the patient distinguish between what he imagines and what he perceives.

The stay-with-it technique illustrates par excellence Perls's emphasis on the role of phobic avoidance in all of neurotic behavior. In his view, the neurotic has habitually avoided vigorous contact with a variety of unpleasant and dysphoric experiences. As a result avoidance has become ingrained, a phobic anxiety has been routinized, and major dimensions of experience have never been adequately mastered.

It is interesting, in this connection, to be reminded of the title of Perls's first book, *Ego, Hunger and Aggression.* The title was chosen carefully to carry the message that we must adopt toward psychological and emotional experiences the same active, coping attitudes that we employ in healthy eating. In healthy eating we bite the food; then we effectively chew, grind, and liquefy it. It is then swallowed, digested, metabolized, and assimilated. In this way we have truly made the food a part of ourselves.

The Gestalt therapist—most especially with the stay-with-it technique—encourages the patient to undertake a similar "chewing up" and painstaking assimilation of emotional dimensions of life that have hitherto been unpleasant to the taste, difficult to swallow, and impossible to digest. In this way the patient gains improved self-confidence and a far greater capacity for autonomy and for dealing energetically with the inevitable frustrations of living.

chapter 6
EXPERIENTIAL PSYCHOTHERAPY WITH FAMILIES*

Walter Kempler

Upon two commandments hangs all the law on which experiential psychotherapy with females stands: (1) attention to the current interaction as the pivotal point for all awareness and interventions, and (2) involvement of the total therapist-person, who brings overtly and richly his full personal impact on the families with whom he works—not merely a bag of tricks called therapeutic skills. While many therapists espouse such fundamentals, in actual practice there is a tendency to hedge on this biprincipled commitment. This paper is offered as a hedge-clipper.

The extant interaction—the current encounter—demands constant vigil. It means attention to the here and now, not to the exclusion of past and future but to the extent that any pertinent deviation from the here and now be considered a transient, although necessary, diversion, and that each detour be succinct and promptly integrated into the current interaction.

* Originally published in *Family Process*, 1968, 7, 88–89. Reprinted with the permission of the author, The Mental Research Institute, and The Family Institute.

For example, a mother, father, and their eight-year-old daughter are embroiled in a discussion about the daughter's behavior. The father, clearly and firmly, contends that the daughter is quite able to express herself, while the mother contends that she never speaks up in her own behalf and needs help on this matter. The therapist, believing direct confrontation is preferable whenever possible, urges the mother to explore her concern with her daughter rather than gossip with the father about her.

M.: [*to daughter*] I wish you could speak freely with us about anything you want [*with obvious condescension*]. It's so important for you to be able to do that.

D.: [*readily*] I say what I want.

M.: Oh no, you don't. You should be able to say anything you wish.

D.: [*again easily*] I do.

M.: [*ignoring her comment*] I wish you did.

T.: [*to mother*] You ignore her remarks.

M.: [*to therapist*] I do because I know I'm right.

T.: [*attempting to assist them to bridge their distance and negotiate anew*] Can you give her an example?

M.: I don't think she's saying here what she wants to.

T.: For instance? [*The therapist does not perceive or share the mother's concern but wishes to give her the opportunity to explore further.*]

M.: That she thinks we are bad parents. For instance, we don't let her speak about what she doesn't like about us . . . like my husband's yelling and maybe my crying bothers her.

T.: [*now that mother is more specific*] Check those out with her.

[*Mother inquires.*]

D.: I don't like Daddy's yelling, but it doesn't bother me too much except when it's to me. I've told him. And it doesn't bother me to see you cry. It used to, but you do so much of it I don't pay attention to it any more.

To this the mother shakes her head sadly as if to say, "I know you're suffering, poor child—if I could only help you know how you are suffering."

The therapist, the father, and the daughter are now all convinced that the daughter isn't suffering—at least not in this area. The therapist offers this to the mother and urges her to consider this information. She ponders awhile and finally says, "I know what it's like to be constantly shut up. It's terrible."

She has left the here and now and returned to her own childhood. She is in the "there and then" so to speak; her current awareness has gone to another time. The therapist encourages her to stay there by saying, "Could you be the little girl now?" She already is. The therapist is merely permitting her to openly acknowledge it. "Close your eyes and speak to your parents about what it's like to be constantly shut up."

The mother closes her eyes and begins crying. The therapist says, "Talk to them."

After sobbing a while, the mother speaks with her eyes closed: "Oh Mother, if only you knew. I don't think you ever knew. [*Cries more heavily*] I could never tell you anything. And it wasn't even all bad. I just wanted you to listen to me—just once—just let me say what's on my mind." She continues speaking to her mother in fantasy (her reality of the moment), citing an instance that was particularly painful to her.

When she seemed finished, the therapist suggested she respond as though she were now her mother. This was a novel idea to her. As she began to explore, she found herself at first apologizing by pleading ignorance, and as she continued, now as her own mother, she began defending her right not to listen; then, in tears, explained how inadequate she felt as a mother so she dared not listen.

With this awareness, she at once became the child again, sobbing heavily, exclaiming, "I never knew. That never occured to me. I never knew. I thought you didn't like me. That's what was so terrible. I never thought it was you—that you *couldn't* listen. I just thought you weren't interested. Oh, how horrible it must have been for you. I feel that way too so much of the time (*now she is becoming the parent-mother of today and the crying stops*). That's why I keep telling Cathy [her daughter] to speak up. She does, you know, better than I could."

During this work, the mother reunited parts of her own psyche that had become estranged during her own growing up. When she finished, she looked pensive and fell silent, staring at an empty chair. A meditative silence often follows important cognitions, as though the psychic apparatus needs to be allowed time for reorganization.

After several minutes of comfortable silence had passed, the mother began to move and look about. The therapist, wanting the experience integrated into her current world, urged her to speak to her daughter.

The mother, smiling now, says, "I'm not as bad a mother as you may think—I guess it's more accurate to say 'as I thought I was.' You know, you do speak up much better than I ever did."

The daughter smiles. Their encounter seems completed. The father is then invited to respond. To the therapist, he begins, "I knew I was right but I never thought . . ."

The therapist, interrupting, suggests that he speak to his wife. The father turns to her and continues, "I never thought about what was going on. It just made me angry to see the way you nagged at her. That feeling is all gone now. If you start nagging again, it will probably come back, but I sure feel different about you right now."

The mother replies, "I feel so relieved about all this. I'm sorry I've been such a pill."

The father, doing some work for himself, ignores her apology and says, "Well, maybe I can be more helpful to you in the future if you should get upset again about Cathy."

They fall silent. The therapist feels he has finished with father and daughter; to complete his business of the moment with the mother, he adds, "I didn't like your apology. You needn't be the perfect wife, either."

History-taking, ruminating about genetic derivatives to current behavior, discussion about the *why* of behavior are all antithetical to this approach. Attention to the subject matter of any encounter is considered necessary for launching an encounter. It is best jettisoned, however, as quickly as possible to make way for an experience that exposes to awareness what we do to each other and how we do it. Briefly, the *what* and *how* of behavior displaces the *why;* experiences displace discussion.

When a family arrives, the therapist observes how this family appears, how they impinge on him. Does anxiety prevail in one or more of them? What are they doing? How do they come in? Does the father usher his family in or is he one of the ducklings? What is their mood? Does the therapist like the looks of them? Are they friendly with each other?

The therapist's potential awareness about what he sees is infinite and, of course, colored by his own needs of the moment. He may greet the family much as a good host, smiling and offering his hand, and may begin by introducing himself if a family member has not already done so. Whatever his awareness, hopefully, the therapist approaches the family, curious about what they want from him, interested in how they go about seeking what they need, and ready to engage them with his feelings of the moment.

One family member may begin the verbal exchange. If not, the therapist is obliged to initiate it. Opening statements (like interventions in general) are considered best when they are an "I" statement that identifies the therapist in the here and now, such as an observation about himself: "I'm almost ready for you people. I'm still thinking about the previous session which was quite moving." And if that is not sufficient to complete his departure from the prior hour, a further comment of his current residual would be considered appropriate. The therapist is obliged, not merely urged, to clear himself so that he may be in the present more completely.

His awareness may now go to someone's restlessness, an unusual hair style, or an attractive article of clothing. An opening comment acknowledging such awareness is preferred to a studied silence or a trite question that is not self-disclosing such as "And how are you today?" or "What can I do to help you?" Trivial as this may seem, a self-disclosing atmosphere is best created by example, and the opening statement is an excellent place to begin. In these initial moments of therapy, the therapist serves primarily as a catalyst striving to encourage negotiations among family members. Later, the therapist becomes, at times, a principal in the fray.

"I'd like you to meet my family," a mother may begin, introducing her two sons, Daryl, 15, and Steve, 12, and then her husband, who trails in, unsmilingly offers his hand, grunts courteously, and heads for a chair, obviously a reluctant, dragged-in dragon.

Everyone sits, and during the initial moments of silent settling, the mother, smiling, visually checks out each member of her family and then looks at the therapist as if to say "I'm ready." The children watch the therapist or look about the office. The father visually alternates between therapist and wife, finally settling on his wife. In the brief silence, the mother speaks to the therapist, "Where would you like us to begin?"

Avoiding a question such as "Where would *you* like to begin?" he sets a good example: he says what he wants. "Since you seem most ready to engage, I would suggest you begin by telling each member of your family what you do not like about living with him." He could have intensified the encounter at the outset by directing attention to the dissimilarity of the mother and father in their readiness to lead and engage. Preferring a softer opening, the therapist accepts the mother's readiness to begin and moves to create an engagement within the family.

But the mother responds by turning to the father, asking him, "Do you want to start?" Ignoring the therapist's suggestion, she invites the father's leadership. Leading with a question is generally not engagement but rather an attempt to remain obscure, hoping someone else will initiate the interaction. By turning to her husband after the therapist's instruction, she confirms that, at least in part, this is her intention. The therapist now suspects she knows very well where she would like to begin.

The father replies, "You've started. Go ahead."

The therapist notes that an excuse has been given ("you've started") and a rather feeble one at that—a fact which both ignore—as the mother, now with the father's assertion and the therapist's direction, readily begins.

M.: Our trouble has been mostly with Steve . . .
T.: [*interrupting*] Tell him what you don't like about his behavior.
M.: He knows very well what I don't like. It doesn't help to tell him.
T.: Then I suggest you consult your husband. That's what husbands and wives are for.
M.: I know. I've talked to him but he's not interested.
T.: Then I suggest you discuss *that* with your husband.
M.: I have but when I do he either ignores me or just gets mad at the kids and spanks them. And I don't think that's the way to handle it.
T.: Tell him.
M.: I do. He won't listen to me.
T.: Then discuss that with him.

Her mood suddenly changes from casual and conversational to sadness. She stares at the floor saying "It's no use," and falls silent, withdrawing from the encounter. Her casual conversational posture was acceptable to share with us but to her, obviously, her sadness was not. Since feelings are the cushions of encountering that keep us from crashing into others and breaking, by curbing her feelings of the moment, she has converted this most valuable coping equipment into a wall that inhibits rather than enhances further negotiation. Bringing her nonverbal behavior into the verbal arena can restore the encounter.

T.: I would like to know how you feel right now.

M.: [*without looking up*] Sad and hopeless.

T.: [*attending the obstacle rather than the sadness, since this is her observable behavior*] Sharing your sadness and hopelessness with us seems difficult for you. [*The invitation is accepted and she begins crying softly.*] Now let's hear the words that go with the tears.

The mother shakes her head evidencing a clear "No." The therapist decides not to push further at this time. Even though reluctant to continue, she is, in this moment, more negotiable than father. The therapist's attention turns to him.

T.: You sit silently. I'd like to know where you are now.

F.: [*ignoring mother's sadness and criticism of him, he responds on his safest ground*] I tell the kids to listen to her.

M.: [*angrily to father through her tearfulness*] But you're not effective. They don't listen to you either and then you blow up at them. That's not the way to treat kids. You can't be hitting them all the time.

F.: [*whining*] You always stop me. They'd listen to me, but they know you'll come in and stop me.

T.: You're whining at your wife.

F.: What else can I do? She stops me at every turn.

Until now the therapist has been a catalyst. However, he may be getting annoyed with the husband who transiently engages with his wife and then retreats to the posture of a whimpering child. He may also be annoyed with the wife who double-binds her husband by asking him to be the father, while treating him as a child. The therapist's attention, however, goes to the encounter. The wife is ready to engage but her husband is not. The therapist's attention then must go to him in order to bring him to a negotiating posture. To do this, he now must engage more vigorously and become a principal. There are several ways he can do this.

Should he sense that the father is fragile and truly needs a good mother, the therapist is likely to become one by remaining at a content level and suggesting, for instance, that the father stop whimpering, take his rightful place as leader in his family, and demand from his wife the behavior he requires to enjoy his home. This backing may be given by specific suggestions, such as advising him to demand from his wife that she settle her problems with the children instead of saving them up for him, or by the therapist's vigorously confronting the wife himself by way of example.

Whenever possible, however, the patient should do his own work. Should the therapist conclude that the person (in this instance, the husband) is capable of an oppositional engagement—as indeed he assumes from the report of this father's angrily spanking his children on occasion—then this opportunity for the father to experience his power with adults should not be denied him. The therapeutic task is to bring this available power into the husband's relationship with his wife. The therapist can best do this by directing his own angry frustration into a vigorous attack on this man's whimpering posture.

Before going further, a word is needed about the transition from catalyst or interloper to a more active participant. This transition is largely related to the therapist's needs—his frustration and how he directs his frustration.

In an existential model, the therapist does not suffer from a need for "objectivity." He knows that this concept of the immaculate perception is a myth and that at every moment he is subjective. He believes that therapeutic interventions are most appropriate when they are the richest possible distillation of the therapist's presence. It is not necessary to justify or explain one's behavior in terms of an existing theory so that it may be labeled scientific. In a therapeutic encounter the existence of the therapist-person is more pertinent than the existence of a supportive theory.

The word *spontaneous* may be applied to such behavior. However, it is incumbent on any therapist, existential or not, to distinguish clearly within himself the difference between spontaneous and impulsive behavior. Impulsive behavior is not a thorough representation of a person but rather a fractional escape of behavior in a constricted individual.

For this therapist, frustration leads to action and to further engagement with people. For each therapist the intensity and direction will vary. Those who become passive in the face of their frustration are not likely to become experiential family psychotherapists. They are not likely to become family therapists at all. *Family therapy requires active participation if the therapist is to survive.*

The husband in the case above has now whimpered

at his wife and, when confronted by the therapist, whimpers at him also, helplessly asking, "What can I do? She stops me at every turn."

T.: [*sarcastically, to provoke him*] You poor thing, overpowered by that terrible lady over there.

F.: [*ducking*] She means well.

T.: You're whimpering at me, and I can't stand to see a grown man whimpering.

F.: [*firmer*] I tell you I don't know what to do.

T.: Like hell you don't [*offering and at the same time pushing*]. You know as well as I that if you want her off your back, you just have to tell her to get the hell off your back and mean it. That's one thing you could do instead of that mealy-mouthed apology: "She means well."

F.: [*looks quizzical; obviously he is not sure if he wants to chance it with either wife or therapist, but is reluctant to retreat to the whimpering-child posture again*] I'm not used to talking that way to people.

T.: Then you'd better get used to it. You're going to have to shape up this family into a group that's worth living with, instead of a menagerie where your job is to come in periodically and crack the whip on the little wild animals.

F.: You sure paint a bad picture.

T.: If I'm wrong, be man enough to disagree with me, and don't wait to get outside of here to whimper to your wife about how you didn't know what to say here.

F.: [*visibly bristling and speaking more forcefully*] I don't know that you're wrong about what you're saying.

T.: But now do you like what I'm saying?

F.: I don't. Nor do I like the way you're going about things either.

T.: I don't like the way you're going about things either.

F.: There must be a more friendly way than this.

T.: Sure, you know, whimper.

F.: [*with deliberate softness*] You're really a pusher, aren't you?

T.: How do you like me?

F.: I don't.

T.: You keep forgetting to say that part of your message. I can see it all over you, but you never say it.

F.: [*finally in anger*] I'll say what I damn please. You're not going to tell me how to talk . . . and how do you like that? [*He socks his hand.*]

T.: I like it a helluva lot better than your whimpering. What is your hand saying?

F.: I'd like to punch you right in the nose, I suppose.

T.: You suppose?

F.: [*firmly*] Enough. Get off my back and stay off.

T.: [*delighted to see his assertion*] Great. Now, about the rest of them (*waving to his family*). I'd like you to see if there's anything you'd like to say to them.

F.: [*looks at each of them then settles on his wife*] He's right. I take an awful lot of nonsense from you and I hate it [*still socking his hand*]. I don't intend to take any more. I'll settle with the kids my way. If you don't like it, that's too bad.

His wife says nothing. The children look pleased. The therapist wonders if he will be too harsh on the children but thinks that if he has his power with her, less will spill over onto the children. The father is no longer socking his hand. He sits up straight for the first time and sits back in the chair looking over his family.

T.: What do you kids think about all this?
S.: Okay. [*He looks comfortable.*]
T.: Do you want to come back?
S.: It's okay with me.
T.: Daryl?
D.: I think it's helpful. [*He looks proudly at his father without saying anything but is obviously pleased.*]

The therapist, also pleased with what he sees, tells the father, "I like you better when you are being the man I know you are. I had the fleeting thought that maybe you will become a tyrant, but I know you won't. I'm not afraid of your power. I saw you taste it here and use it very justly with us."

The father doesn't answer. When the therapist inquires about further visits, the father answers without consulting his wife. "We'd better have a couple more."

On the few subsequent visits, the father ushered his family in.

In this approach, the therapist becomes a family member during the interviews, participating as fully as he is able, hopefully available for appreciation and criticism as well as dispensing it. He laughs, cries, and rages. He feels and shares his embarrassments, confusions, and helplessness. He shares his fears of revealing himself when these feelings are a part of his current total person. He sometimes cannot share himself, and hopefully he is able to say at least that much.

One practical consequence of such negotiating with families, then, is the therapist's lack of concern with "taking sides." On the contrary, it is more suspicious when he is never on a side. A feeling therapist often has a side and is comfortable with it. Hopefully, he is sensitive to his own needs. If he is, he will find himself changing sides often enough to be inspiring to everyone. If not, the family will let him know, provided he has clearly established an atmosphere conducive to free exchange.

Another family of mother, father, and twenty-one-year-old daughter are seen for the first time. The daughter has just been released from a psychiatric hospital, where she was briefly hospitalized with the label of an acute psychotic reaction. At present she is at home, heavily tranquilized, spending most of her time in bed.

The mother begins (as seems remarkably usual) with the aforementioned story. She not only begins but she never ends. Her excited, charm-laden loquaciousness is occasionally interspersed with remarks to her husband, such as "Isn't that so dear?" or "What do you think?" She never waits for an answer but babbles on. The therapist is the only one apparently annoyed enough to object. "Oh, I do talk a lot I know. Why don't one of you (turning to husband and daughter) say something?" Before they can, she is off and running again.

This time the therapist tells her to be quiet and invites the father to comment on the babbling. "Oh, she's like that all the time. I'm used to it." Then he offers the observation, "All our daughter needs is a good job. I tell her that all the time but she won't listen." The mother picks up on this and verbally runs nowhere with it. The father permits it.

After several more futile attempts to invite each of them, including the daughter (who remains silent), to look at their behavior and consider altering their encounter-diminishing behaviors, the therapist with great exasperation turns on both parents, telling them in no uncertain terms of their destructive behavior: the mother's incessant babbling, the father's absurd tolerance of it, and further, the absence of any constructive working with each other.

At the end of the therapist's harangue, the daughter smilingly speaks for the first time. "We should have had you when I was ten years old." With some residual grouchiness, the therapist retorts, "But you're not ten now, so get started changing things for yourself."

The mother and father both cheered. Therapy had begun with the therapist siding twice in this first encounter. Within two months, the daughter was working. At three months, therapy had terminated by consensus, and a year later, the therapist was invited to attend the daughter's wedding.

There is no obscuring of the therapist behind a title. He brings his personality and life experiences to the family encounter. It is his uniqueness in this family (he is not likely to be caught up in its painful, interlocking behavior patterns—at least not initially) and his willingness to engage fully with others that are his most valuable therapeutic "techniques." In other words, in experiential psychotherapy within families, there are no "techniques," only people. At every turn, the therapist is obliged to struggle for his right to be seen as he perceives himself, and not to permit distortions such as, for instance, an implication that he is all-knowing or all-powerful. By such example, the family members are likewise encouraged to struggle for what they perceive as their identities. It is during the vigorous clarification of who we are to each other that therapy occurs.

The illustrative samples are admittedly one-dimensional. This seems necessary for clarity of exposition. However, this should not prevent translating the basic principles to more complex moments in therapy when many needs seem to arise at once or when chaos seems temporarily to prevail. At such moments, it behooves the experientially oriented family therapist to turn to his own needs first. Perhaps he will demand a moment's moratorium from bedlam in order to see in which direction he arbitrarily wishes to proceed. Possibly he will request some assistance from the working family in this matter. His own transient uncertainty is a welcome expression in a good experientially-oriented family encounter.

chapter 7

ANNE: Gestalt Techniques with a Woman with Expressive Difficulties

Joen Fagan

Anne was a twenty-eight-year-old student, married, with two children, who enrolled in my class in Abnormal Psychology. She did nothing that would call attention to her until the first test. She showed a high degree of mastery of material and clear indications of intuitive sensitivity, but expressed her ideas in extremely poor English with many errors in grammar, spelling, and punctuation. Her second test presented even more impressive evidence of her ability—and of her expressive handicap.

(Marasmus) a reactions of infants who are deprived of maternial affection, a severe physical conditions resulting in body and mental deteriation
(Undoing) an ego-defense mechanism characterized by a effort to atone for undesirable thoughts or impules. Like a child we are taught to apoligizes type of constance apoligizing to make things right.
(Parkinson's symptoms) A brain disease of unknown orgin, the patient has rythumic tremurs, difficulties with gait. No loss of mental ability but lose of ability to make muscles do what the patient desires.
(Korsakoff's syndrome) In chronic alcoholics and senile pyschoes, the patient has poor memory and uses conflagulation.
(Huntington's chorea) A brain disease of unknown order which a pre-senile deteriotion of the brain. Only brain disease which follows Mendle's gentics. Patient has jerky involintory tremers. Mental deteriotation.

Fig. 1. Examples of Anne's Test Answers

After the second test, I suggested a conference. Both pleased and frightened by my interest, Anne wrote me a letter to say that she also had difficulty in talking about her problem. She did come, however, and indicated in a hesitant, apologetic way that her inability to spell and express herself clearly and correctly had existed since the first grade. Neither her own efforts, spurred by her continued embarrassment and considerable tutoring, nor a year of psychotherapy had resulted in any noticeable improvements.

Since I perceived that her high potential in many areas was clearly handicapped by her problems in expressing her abilities, I asked if she wished to participate in an experiment that would consist of a series of tasks that she would perform by herself with minimal direction from me. While I could not guarantee that this would help her, her past lack of success at getting help through the usual channels suggested that there was little to lose. Anne agreed eagerly, and arrangements were made to begin the following quarter.

In Anne's diary of her experiences, she describes in detail the instructions and techniques that were used. Briefly, the tasks were:

1. Write in free association style your thoughts about *play*.
2. Look up in an unabridged dictionary, the derivation of the following words: *tantalize, prejudice, agony, gentle, responsible, devil, fool.*
3. Write your associations to *anxiety*.
4. Draw or copy a picture, first with your right, then with your left hand.

5. Write ten reasons why people should not obey rules, misspelling every word.
6. Write your associations to *anger*.
7. Read poetry selections aloud.
8. Finger-paint left-handed.
9. Listen to a tape (selections sung by Leontyne Price) and write what you hear.
10. Listen to a tape (orchestral selections) and finger-paint with your left hand.
11. Listen to a tape (orchestral) and write your emotional responses in adjectives.
12. Study a flower intensely and then finger-paint it.
13. Write three criticisms of other people and five of yourself.

Each task was designed to be completed in a thirty-minute session; sessions were twice a week. While several other tasks had been intended, Anne had to stop the experiment prematurely so they could not be included. (It is also clear from the diary that the tasks had fulfilled much of their purpose and might have been discontinued, even had the interruption not occurred.)

The general procedure of self-experimentation was based on Perls's *Gestalt Therapy*, which describes a series of instructions the student reads and follows, the purpose being to increase his awareness of his sensory, visceral, perceptual, emotional, and motoric functioning. The specific tasks I chose came from several sources. Those involving drawing, painting, and emphasis on the right-left dichotomy were based on techniques and procedures used by Perls in his workshops at Esalen Institute. The use of free-association writing was modified from Hayakawa* to assist in freeing written expression.

The use of the self-experiment procedure was chosen for a number of reasons: (1) my knowledge of the power of such methods; (2) evidence of the failure of more direct or specific approaches with Anne; (3) my perception of Anne was being so blocked by other people's actual or potential evaluations that she could get most from a situation where she was in charge with no external evaluations, only clearly implied support and interest; (4) limitations on my time; (5) the opportunity to test the power of Gestalt techniques in a challenging situation; and (6) my wish to assist this potentially able person. While I was aware of the possibility that some organic damage might have been partially responsible for Anne's expressive problem, there seemed more to be gained by viewing her problem as modifiable.

The specific tasks were chosen partly for theoretical or dynamic reasons, partly from hunch. It seemed that Anne's failure to "follow the rules" was related to an inability to rebel more openly, to express anger or say "no" more directly. It was apparent that she perceived and projected much criticism from others and criticized herself severely. Almost any form of expression was a painful and anxiety-producing event for her, with words being perceived as difficult, demanding, immovable objects rather than actual or potential objects of play or beauty. These thoughts helped determine the selection of the tasks involving writing. I also wanted the first few tasks to have "face validity" for

* Hayakawa, S. I. Learning to think and to write: Semantics in freshman English. *ETC.*, 1962, 18, 419–426.

her and to be neutral emotionally. The tasks involving noncognitive expressiveness were chosen because of my perception of Anne as a blocked and tightly bound woman whose prime difficulty was in expression in a global sense. Listening, looking, touching, moving, and the combination of these were utilized in a number of tasks with the hope that some sense modality would be relatively more open and could be used to tap into the area where her feelings and responsiveness were buried. The use of the left hand in a number of tasks was based on Perls's ideas about the right-left split. I hoped also to encourage her to stop thinking of her responses as having to be "right." The goal of all the techiques was to increase Anne's sensory awareness, emotional responsiveness, motoric expressiveness, and personal integration. If this could be accomplished, then it was hypothesized that the more specific spelling and grammatical problems would tend to solve themselves.

The diary that follows was begun spontaneously by Anne at the start of the experiment. She did not tell me she was keeping it until a number of weeks later, and showed me the first part only toward the end of the experiment. The diary has received minimal editing, with spelling corrections made for ease of reading; some sections were deleted because of being unrelated to the experiment, embarrassing to Anne, or identifying of her or others.

As Anne's account of her experiences begins, it is obvious how hard she tried to get the instructions right, to follow them exactly, and to do what was expected of her. Another major theme is her frequent effort to find reasons and explanations for the tasks —usually totally incorrect. Only as more sensory involvement and "body" entered did she become aware of her own responses and find meaning "inside." It is likely that the first few tasks did build a base of support that facilitated the later release. The unblocking of Anne's sensory and emotional responsiveness was closely followed by her wish for more direct contact with me, and the ability to express herself more directly to me, her husband, and others.

As far as specific accomplishments, there was some improvement in Anne's written expression before the end of the quarter in which the experiment was conducted. Her spelling and ability to express herself in writing have continued to improve and now fall within the normal range for college graduates. Three months after the experiment, Anne went back into therapy and was able to make much fuller use of it. (She had terminated therapy earlier because of her inability to tell her therapist her feelings about him.) She has since graduated from college and has made a much more adequate adjustment in all aspects of her life. She has pursued in a determined way her area of special interest and has made some considerable contributions, her recent work demonstrating ingenuity and clear indications of creativity.

I am more than satisfied with the results of the experiment with Anne. In considering the factors that produced the change, I see several of major importance. It is obvious that Anne had strong motivation to change, but this had existed for many years. It is also obvious that I became a very important person to her, toward whom she had strong positive feelings. However, she had had similar feelings toward her therapist, and her earlier response had been to leave therapy because of her inability to express and explore these. I am certain that my clear interest in her and my appreciation of her potentialities were communicated to her, but the actual amount of time I spent in talking with her during the previous quarter and the first four weeks of the experiment did not exceed a total of thirty minutes. Finally, the techniques used facilitated emotional unblocking and acted as catalysts for change. In the final analysis, all of the above factors probably contributed to the growth that is so apparent in the diary.

As I reread Anne's diary, I find that the experiment itself, Anne's response to specific tasks, and my own role fade into the background. I become most aware of a person, initially frozen into immobility, who slowly, then rapidly, begins to grow with a vividness and excitement that I find breathtaking and awesome —and which leaves me with renewed faith in human courage and human possibilities. Anne's diary, in my final judgment, is less an example of Gestalt techniques than a testimonial to human capacity for growth.

Anne's Diary*

This is the story of a girl (she was really a woman, but she didn't know how to behave like one) who had a problem (well, actually she had quite a few problems, but one particular one which was extremely apparent) and what helped this girl become a woman and to overcome some of her problems.

It all began when this girl was in an Abnormal Psychology class. Now the problem that this girl had

* The diary was originally titled, "Diary of a Girl with Blue Paint on Her Nose." The introduction was written at the end of the quarter, after the rest of the diary was finished. Some spelling corrections have been made for easier reading.

which was so apparent was a spelling problem. This spelling problem greatly hindered her in her school work. However this particular teacher tried to see what the student was trying to say rather than just how she was able to say (or spell) it. On the second test in this course, this girl made a 98, now that's a pretty high grade for anyone, but for a girl who can't spell it's not only high it's downright remarkable. The teacher had written on this paper. "How about that?" and "Please see me." After class the girl went up to see the teacher.

G.: "You wanted to see me?"
T.: "Yes, what are we going to do about your spelling problem?"
G.: "Well, I guess teachers have been wondering that since I was in the first grade."

The girl thanked the teacher for not counting off for the spelling errors. The teacher said come and talk to me some time. But the teacher didn't know that one of this girl's other problems was that she couldn't talk, particularly about her problems.

The girl decided to write the teacher a letter explaining the problem and why she couldn't talk about it. This is the letter:

Dear Dr. Fagan,

Although my problem to a great extent centers around writing, I find it much easier to write about than to talk about. In fact any close emotional problem is very difficult for me to communicate, written or verbally, my feelings on the subject. I usually become silent. I withdraw because the stress that I experience when placed again in the frustrating position of explaining my problem is too great for me to cope with.

The problem when it is in its full glory includes not just spelling, but grammar, coherence of thoughts, reading comprehension, and great verbal expression. There have been times when I could not write a coherent sentence. There have been times when speaking was so difficult that I could only mutter a halting, faltering statement. Under stress I use the wrong words, mix words up, or combine them in an unheard of fashion.

I want very much to be able to completely overcome these difficulties, but I do not know what else to do. I have really come a long way. Spelling is the last stronghold which I cannot break through. I have almost decided to let this ride and hope that as each part of me experiences growth, spelling like the caboose on a train will come tagging along, making progress but at a slower pace.

I could give you reasons and explanations about this problem, but they are long and drawn out. After I finished telling them, I would still have my problem. I do not know why I have this problem or why I cannot get rid of it.

I appreciate your interest in me. My first reaction was that you probably do not have time to talk with me. When you can, I would like to talk with you, but you have to realize the extreme fear I have for this subject. I have experienced shame and guilt, I have tried to cover up, hide, change, but it's still there.

You have probably known that there is more involved here than just the overt symptoms. I have only a few suggestions that might over the years help me. If I could feel that people would accept me with my problem (just like one who stutters or who has a tic), if I could feel that I am enough of a person not to be destroyed by criticism or ridicule, if I can become an achiever rather than a nonachiever, if I could feel that I am not going to be discriminated against because of the particular type (academic) of problem that I have, then I feel that maybe I would not manifest my confusion and anxiety by difficulties in written and verbal communication. I sometimes feel that my brain is a switchboard and I just cannot plug in the right switches for communication.

I have only found a handful of people during my life who had the patience, kindness, and understanding to extend a helping hand to me. Thank you for being one of these people. In my classroom work there has usually been a high correlation between the teacher's ability to understand me and my performance in class.

This is a pretty sick sounding letter, but if I wrote it any other way it wouldn't be real.

Anne

The girl really did not ever expect to talk with the teacher, but after the exam the teacher offered to help the girl next quarter during the break (a "free" forty-minute period in the morning schedule) with her problem. The girl was delighted because there was someone who thought that something could be done about her problem. All during Christmas holidays the girl thought about what was going to be done about her problem. In 1967 at Georgia State College, in the girl's junior year of college, the adventure began. The cure for the spelling problem was to be two thirty-minute sessions a week. These sessions turned into the most traumatic, exciting, miserable, and marvelous adventure this girl had ever entered into. I know so much about this girl, because I am the girl and this is my story.

January 7

I had my first session with Dr. Fagan. I was surprised when she handed me a stack of paper. I had to borrow a pen. She gave me the instructions to write free-association, no regard to grammar, spelling, punctuation. The topic—play. There is no need to restate what I wrote—she has it in a file, although she told me I was writing for myself, and that she would not read what I wrote unless I wanted her to.

I was concerned about not finishing a thought so the next day requested to finish. She said I could and asked why I had not come that day. I had not understood I was to come—thinking she had said Thursday *or* Friday. She laughed and said I was in for the duration.

January 12

I gave Dr. Fagan the completed thought written on a piece of notebook paper. This feeling of incompletion had disturbed me—like a conversation with rapport established and interrupted before completion of thoughts. Phone calls, children, time are interruptions.

My second assignment was a list of words to look up in the dictionary. I was disappointed for I had wanted to write some more, and wondered what subject I would be told to write about.

While looking up the words, I had a funny feeling that I had misunderstood my instructions. She used a word which I assumed was definition.* I need to find out that word.

I looked up the words, reading and writing the

* What I had told her was *derivation,* choosing words (sincere, tantalize, agony, etc.) whose origins illuminate their meaning. I had hoped that she would be able to get some feeling of play in relation to words, but she instead clearly turned the assignment into work. This paralleled her writing about "play" which ended with a disphoric association to sex play.—J.F.

meanings. While only on the fourth word, the bell rang. I read the last two and was unable to look up two of them. I will go back later and look them up.

I went back to pick up my coat and books and reported to Dr. Fagan that I had not completed my task.

ani
this thought distressing I can't even spell it ange anger, tention
frustration I can't make people understand me aniety anxity
an anxiety
I talk with my husband he cannot understand what I am trying to
communicate. I feel tight in side. We have had an arguement every
night this week
I have to deside what I am going to be and be it no one can interfer
with my being
pulled in too many different directions like ropes tied to my hands,
feets being pulled apart
what I have to be and what others need for me to be I know when I hand
someone a paper I have written the errors bother them they laugh at
mistakes or cannot believe I am that incapable of being able to eple
spell or write correctly,
I am ashamed about my writing to test a friend I see if they can stand
the extend of my problem by asking or letting them read something I
have written pass test my husband has not passed, every time I ask
for his help I get a lecture on spelling or basic English he gets angry
I become anxious
School not anxious any more except on test being tested or examined
being judged by my writing I can not get my knowledge on paper
last night arguement with by husband has never like how or way we
live He is thinking of buying new dinning room table this makes me
sick all he wants is a neat well furnished house who is there or what
happened doesn't matter
I am freer from anxiety than used to be When I feel it I try to do
something look at me look at problem - look look look I should not have
left treatment when I did
I feel like I failed Gail I feel never well be a family, have unity or
growth or love or freedom or life husband asked if I had been happy
way we life I had to think of happiness as basied on material item
used to need material china, silver, furniture, pianio I was
miserable
Happeness being free from anie anxeit anxiety happeness people growth
maturity productive work husband fussed at Gail about her spelling
fussed at Robbie for not writing neatly on homework this disturbs me
am I too permissive does growth come from producing anxiety about
problem fussing or growth comes from support you are alright in
enough was that I can over look or help you with you' problems
not as anxious now as when first started writt writing yes I am I am
scared about something don't know what
can't write just think life end nothing sadness work happiness
is someone believing in me struggle fight nag fuss acceptance
success college work which way to go what can I do to free myself
from anxiety
what can I do to solve my problem I am anxious now why subject
writing was I already anxious I hate to read what I write

Fig. 2. Anne's Associations to "Anxiety"

January 15

Again, I went to Dr. Fagan. I felt in a happy mood. I followed her into another office stating that I had completed the list of words. She said I was not to feel that I should complete what I started on these days. She also said not to write using correct style—that I was to free-associate. She assigned me a subject—anxiety.

From the moment she uttered the word, I became anxious and remained so in varying degrees during the entire session. At one point I did not see how I could turn in the paper or go to class. When the bell rang, I was less anxious and very willing to stop.

My sessions with her seem unstructured. I am to come two days a week, but can choose the days. There is something very comfortable about this nonstructured element.

I can't understand why it displeased her that I had continued and finished the words. Since I am doing this to learn and improve my language, I thought this was what I was supposed to do.

January 17

I am angry—I hate to draw. Today Dr. Fagan gave me some colored pencils and told me to draw. She gave me a calendar picture of mountains and valley in either Switzerland or Germany. Fog, mist, color, sunlight, trees, I can't stand to look at my drawings. It was painful to try to get such a beautiful picture on a piece of white paper. I couldn't draw the house. I didn't know how to give the impression of mist, fog. In any other position I would have chucked the whole thing and said I can't draw, but I tried as much as my extreme dislike and lack of ability would allow.

And when I finished all this effort, she gave me another piece of paper to draw with my left hand. I looked at her more astonished than before. And then began the painful task, eagerly awaiting the bell. When I gave her my pictures, she asked if I had compared them. I said no. She said it might be wise if I did sometimes. I do not want to look at the pictures. But I think I know what she is getting at. I have thought I should be left handed. Maybe she thinks so too and feels that some of my language problems come from this.

January 22

Dr. Fagan handed me a dictionary and paper. Her instructions were to write an essay on ten reasons why people should not obey rules and that I should not spell any words right even if I had to look them up to spell them wrong. I laughed and said I doubted if I would need the dictionary.

After my initial surprise over the instructions, I enjoyed misspelling the words and writing about breaking rules. I see two methods behind this, first that I could concentrate on misspelling and possibly begin to be conscious of the way letters are placed and second, that possibly I show my rebellious nature in spelling or rather not spelling. I liked what I said about rules. I reminds me of how pleased I was in my phonetics course to learn how common the errors I make are and some of the reasons behind these errors.

January 25

Today she asked me to get a copy of Milton's *Paradise Lost* and Keats from the library. Then she told me to write on anger, but I couldn't because I was not angry. I felt no anger.

Anger
I ca'nt write about anger. I am not angry happy joy blue mist over
distant mountains
Maybe I misspell because I an angry with people, particularly people
who try to teach me something I learn best by inspiration and wanted
to achieve
Anger, anger · if I can't feel it I can"t write about in this is
interesting because I became anxiety the moment Dr. Fagan spoke
the word but I cannot feel anger
What makes me angry it makes me angry when I can't communicate
with people or they with me I want to take their heads and hold them
in my hands shake them and demand rapport Now I am angry
frustrated because of all the people who would not take the time to
listen to me.
I hate my mother when she says thing like when she views Mark's
old work and new ones she is discussed (disgusted) with the new one
and pronounces them as bad, narrow mind, ignorant she can not
tell good and does'nt want anyone else to either
hard throbbing in head sick feeling in stomach I feel like nothing is
ever going to change weary, tired of struggling anger gets no wear
were people angry with me and I can't trust them how can I be one and
reveal my inner self when all that happens when confronted with this is
lectures and anger What do you do with anger what what what
if you show anger and it is not appropreate you are wrong in dog
house when you keep the anger inside you find other people don't
know how you feel and that even though you put up with them, they
won't put up with you; Anger inside keeps building up up up up and
you want to explode or stop exsisting
half time I feel like a little girl rest of time I feel like a weary old
woman How do I feel when I am angry I don't know. What do I do with
anger. I try to show it when I can, but constantly feel people telling
me this is not allow They say you have to take it from me, but you
can't give it back to us
when you love some one it hurts so much to have them angry with you
but even more for you to be angry with them
What is anger like like a boiling pot on the stove if it spills
someone gets burnt like the wind blowing so hard the branches creake
and breaks off like a child spell stepping on a bug and squashing it
like a bruise on your kee knee black, blue, yellowish in contrast
with white skin
Anger is like having a kin knife in your guts and having it pulled and
pushed until nothing is lift left. Worse than anger is what follows
hollow, pain, nothingness and what to do how to a aee aeh act
how to learn and not let it happen again, but it happens again & again
& again with the same miserable feeling

Fig. 3. Anne's Associations to "Anger"

January 26

I went back again today. I wonder if she was surprised to see me two days in a row. She looked around her files for something, but couldn't find it. I was afraid she was going to ask me to look at the pictures I had drawn. She asked if I had the books, I did—I had brought the Milton from home and had just checked Keats out of the library. She sat down and first marked Milton and then Keats. She handed them back to me and told me to read them aloud until I could do it well. As she unlocked the door to another office I said but it isn't sound proof—she said well you don't have to shout.

So I sat, reading softly aloud. In Milton book 1, *Paradise Lost,* I found two particular passages I liked. I am sure I am reading in my own meanings.

> . . . What in me is dark illumine,
> What is low raise and support:
> . . . One who brings
> A Mind not to be changed by place or time
> The mind is its own place, and in itself
> Can make a heaven of hell, a hell of heaven.
> What matter where, if I be still the same
> And what I should be, all but less than he
> Whom thunder hath made greater? Here at least
> We shall be *free.*

From Keats's "Ode to a Nightingale."

> This not through envy of thy happy lot
> But being too happy in thine happiness.

There were some words I could not pronounce and places where because I did not know the meaning, I could not phrase it right. I read a little past the bell (I plan to do some more later) and I asked Dr. Fagan if I could come tomorrow. She said I could.

January 27

Dr. Fagan suggested that this might be a good time to think about what we had done. I thought she meant for me to write that day my feelings, so I told her I was keeping a diary. I think she was pleased. She said thus far she had avoided any communications about what I felt about what was happening—I said did she want to read my diary? She let me know she wanted me to talk about anything I had been thinking.

First, I asked about the left-handed drawing and told my story about perhaps experiencing a change in dominance. She said this was not what she was indicating or had interest in. She did it because in class this summer in California some drawings had been done left handed and some interesting different approaches had been discovered.

I then brought up something that had bothered me. Since she was working with me and might also teach me, I was afraid if I took a test under her and didn't show some improvement, she might feel her time wasted on me, or feel that her method had failed or something. In my effort to please her I would be under such stress that I wouldn't be able to do anything—she said she had nothing invested in me—I can't remember exactly what she said, but it was trying to help me know that what I did she was not ego-involved in. I said that she was a special person to me right now and I appreciated what she was doing for me and thinking I was worth helping—the only way I knew to show how I felt was by achieving and yet this would place me under stress. I am not sure the exact way the rest of the conversation went, but this is as I remember it —she said on a test to start off and misspell the first couple of sentences deliberately. This surprised me (my, how I use that word, *surprise,* but that's exactly the feeling I get when she says something). I reacted by telling her that I had the feeling while writing the rules that perhaps I had used spelling as a way of rebelling—she smiled at this. I felt I had hit the nail on the head. Only, I continued, when I stopped rebelling I was left with the habit which I couldn't break —she said something about my achieving and my family's achieving—I couldn't get this—and what I said was rather incoherent. She could see I was struggling with it and said that this was something I could not expect to grasp right off.

I said what first came into my mind that mother had not reacted to my making the dean's list. Dr. Fagan told me about a man from the slums who had gotten a Ph.D. and his mother would not believe it. I know this feeling.

She also said that she could read through my spelling errors and see what I was trying to say. This didn't bother her. She wanted me to know, I think, that I should relax, not be under stress and just be me and experience what growth I could.

She said she wanted to help with the problem because she felt it interfered with my doing, expressing what I wanted to. And that's the understatement of the year—I might as well be deaf and blind, or armless and legless.

I told her that I am ashamed for people to see my work. When she let me know our talk was over—I left feeling pretty good.

February 1

She had a box under her arm and paper. Earlier when asked if she were cut she said no, red finger paint. Without being told I followed her. We stopped for water in a coke bottle, after which I carried the papers and we entered the Experimental Psychology

Laboratory. In one of the compartments, she put the paper, paints, coke bottle and paper towels down. She asked if I knew how to finger-paint and I said I had two kids. She said paint left-handed using, if the paints held out, black, blue and red.

I began to paint attempting a dark black and blue cloudy sky with an ocean underneath, but then I realized I was using my right hand. I left that painting and began another—with my left hand. I think I am freer with my left hand, more rigid with my right. So I let go and just smeared paint. Mostly blue, but then I added red and ended with a painting with blue on each side and lavender in the middle. I just swirled, rolled and blended—I wanted a rhythm and grace, but am never able to achieve in art work. I went back and wet the other painting and did one with my left hand. I think a lot more went on in my mind while painting than I am able to remember.

When I finished, I washed up and headed back to take the paints to Dr. Fagan. On the way I met her—she said that I had blue paint on my nose.

February 5

Dr. Fagan brought a tape recorder into another office but couldn't find a plug. I said shall I find an empty room? She said yes and gave me a tape with Nos. 1, 41, 80, etc., written on the box and a handful of paper, and told me to listen to it two times and then write what I had heard. I think she said the first two and that they might not start at exactly on 1 and 40, but I was not sure of the instructions. I thought I would be transcribing and unpleasant memories arose from failing all my German transcriptions.

So off I went to a classroom, plugged in the recorder

—and it was music—how surprised I was and delighted, but I thought I must have not listened to the instructions, so I listened to spots on the tape—all music. I started at the beginning and listened to a girl sing. Was I supposed to write the words or the sounds that I thought I heard? Then I knew that was not it—music is not words, songs are not words, they are only the feeling responses which people experience while listening to them. So I listened, it was breathtaking. I decided for the first time, I would have to go back and tell Dr. Fagan that I found it impossible to do what she said. I wished I could have written my feelings while listening, but I have not developed the ability to express that type of response.

The bell rang and I picked up the recorder thrilled with the music I had heard and excited about it.

February 8

It had been raining and stopped. The day was warm and the skies clear. For some reason it was a particularly lovely. I stood in the hall talking to some students before Dr. Fagan came. She presented me with a set of keys and the same tape I had used Friday. She instructed me to get the recorder from the supply room, pointed to a selection and told me to finger paint with my left hand while listening to the tape. I could hardly help from chuckling and asking should I whistle "Dixie" and write free association with my right hand while stringing beads with my toes? Then I said where is the supply room? She said the door next to the men's rest room. I said shall I put a sign on me? She said no, just don't go in the door marked Men. So off I went, picked up my pocketbook, the bag of materials, the tape and recorder and I couldn't find an empty room.

I decided if I went to Experimental Psychology Laboratory I would waste time. Then I remembered the little room off the women's rest room. If it had a plug in it I was set. It did and after getting the tape on the recorder, the paper wet, and the paints ready, I began. My first thought—how the hell do you paint to music, second thought—how the hell do you paint? I chose red, smeared it over the entire paper. The musical selection was over and another one began which indicated to me I had the tape on the wrong speed—perhaps that's why I chose red.

In the midst of this rather disorganized, ridiculous situation (a 28-year-old woman finger-painting to music in a college rest room; there are probably people who have been locked up for less) I was able to achieve some rather unique and beautiful feelings. The music aroused in me some sensitive, sensuous, exotic feelings which lead me to believe that if I were totally without language, every feeling and emotion could be communicated to me through music. So the music spoke to me and I tried with all my heart to get the rhythm into my left hand and thus onto the paper. I listened again and again each time erasing (by smoothing out) the patterns I had previously stroked through the red paint. How many different times I did this I couldn't say, but I was surged with an intense desire to manipulate that paint in a rhythmic pattern similar to the music. As usual, I was unsuccessful, but the depth of my pleasure was reward enough. I cleaned up, left the painting on the floor and ran to class late.

February 11

Now I have time to sit down and write my feelings about this fascinating therapy Dr. Fagan has involved me in. Since I had a test today, I studied yesterday rather than take time to write. I can only say I am happy, pleased, and rather delighted to be writing again.

Before describing the last session I must go back and write some of the remarkable discoveries, or revelations which occurred to me since Monday's session. Either this first discovery is so basic that everyone already knows it, or it is so foolish that no one is impressed by it. I am inspired by the discovery. It began when I wanted to bring back the music I had listened to. The tune couldn't come nor the rhythm—but when I moved my left hand in the patterns (or to the music) which I had attempted to blend into the paint, the total sounds of the music came to me. I discovered the way I remember music (perhaps other things too) is not by intonation or the rhythm but by the patterns—the patterns of music. A combination of patterns of feelings, volume, tone, tune, rhythm. I can't really say why this is so fascinating to me except that now that I have identified it, it facilitates my use of it. Not too long ago after seeing the movie *Lilith,* I was impressed with the music, particularly the theme, but couldn't at a given moment recall (bring back the music). It would just occur to me (sometimes at rather unpredictable times) and then it would be gone. Once when I remembered it, I said I must do something to facilitate my being able to bring back the music when I want to. So I chose five descending notes, by remembering this scale, I thought I was using intonation as a memory device, but what I was doing was remembering a pattern and through this pattern the rest of the music came. So I had used a device which I myself had identified. It worked and does work because with both sets of music I am able to completely recall every aspect.

The second discovery has probably a more personal intent. Quite a few years ago, I placed my violin softly on its case and snapped the locks shut—I don't want this to sound soapy—I am not implying by this that the world or community lost something when I reached the decision to play no more, or that anything would be gained by my going back to it. I did not play well, but I loved my violin, I struggled with it, the rewards involved were totally personal. I still am not at the point in written expression that I could adequately explain what playing the violin alone or in an orchestra did for me. Somehow it filled a tremendous gap (void). When I made the decision to put it up, to play no more, it was painful, like part of me dying and no one, not a living soul, knew the depths of my loss. So the conclusion I arrived at is that I cannot take a part of me which has meaning to me, which fills a need, and decide that it no longer exists or that it can be packed in a case and the locks snapped. I think I have quite a few cases to go back and unsnap, unlock and reexplore.

When Dr. Fagan first mentioned my problem to me —she handed back a test with a "please see me" written on it. Then she said something that really hit me —I may have mentioned it before, but if so it has reoccurred to me—"What are we going to do about your spelling?"—not how did I get this way or why hadn't I done something about it.

There are other ideas running through my head, but not clearly. Somehow the freedom with which I moved the paints to the music made me feel that I had never been that free with emotions, so as my emotions were confused, distorted (lacked perceptions) and flowed in uneven jerks—so my communications developed along the same lines.

The thing I hate most is to be wrong and yet I have spent my whole life being wrong. Did I or do I have the need to be wrong? If so, when I do not need that any longer, will not my communications clear?

February 11

The questions is why was this particular session so intense for me? It could be that I started my answer in the previous paragraphs. Maybe I had more invested in this (one almost missed, or particularly granted) session. Verbally she said (while handing me the keys) listen to this and write only adjectives or feelings. But somehow I think I received more communication than that. It was as if she were asking me to allow myself full emotional exposure to every feeling that the music conveyed to me. I got the recorder and tried two rooms, but the recorder wouldn't work. I had on a sweater, I was getting hot, the recorder was heavy, and I had my pocketbook and notebook. I decided maybe the wall outlets weren't working, so returned to the little room off the restroom. Still would not work, I was almost on the verge of getting Dr. Fagan to help me when I discovered that there were two off-on switches. So, I sat on the floor and listened. Why was that experience so intense—why did that music speak to me so—why, why, why? There are no words in the English language to really describe it. I experienced a wide range of emotions in an intense degree. It was like experiencing all at once every type of emotion I had ever felt. The height of ecstasy and the depth of miserable confusion and pain. I made an inadequate list of adjectives and feelings. When the bell rang, there were tears in my eyes, I experienced a complete inability to control myself and a feeling of being extremely vulnerable.

I just couldn't come back. I put up the recorder. When I walked down the hall, Dr. Fagan was at her door. I couldn't look up, when I feel this vulnerable I can't let anyone see me. I handed her the keys, tape, and paper and walked to pick up my books. And then something tremendous happened. Dr. Fagan began whistling the music I had just listened to—I did an about-face and entered her office. This was just the link I needed to be able to go in and risk exposing my emotions. I asked would you like to hear a few discoveries I made Monday? She said sure. She really looked so pleased, I was almost sorry I had not made more of an effort at communicating with her before. So I told her about the patterns of music and about her saying what can *we* do about your spelling. The experience that I had just been through had so shaken me that I spoke in a faltering voice. I was unable to determine what effect I had on her. I lowered my head and said those are just a few of the discoveries.

All during the class which followed, I was withdrawn. I had experienced something I couldn't handle, cope with. I could not come back, I could not look at people.

February 13 (Saturday)

Friday my husband and I had a particularly meaningful, inspirational talk. I can't remember all of it, but I did tell him about my experience Thursday. After a while he commented that he thought he saw what Dr. Fagan was trying to do for me. Then later he commented maybe many of my problems stem from a frustrated creativity. I don't think ever in our married life has he in one evening been so close to grasping some concept of me.

February 15

I was extremely excited this morning. While waiting for Dr. Fagan, the secretaries asked me what I did. They didn't believe me and tried to say I was taking a reading course. I tried to explain some of the things happening to me, but I don't think they really understood. Dr. Fagan walked up—the place was cold and she began putting on her coat. She looked in the other office saying someone had taken her chair. She asked me to come into her office and I did. She handed me a daffodil. I can't remember ever before being handed a single flower. She told me to Zen it. (I knew this had something to do with Zen Buddhism, but I have not read a book on the subject—I must do so soon.) I said "What?" I looked at her and I think we were both a little amused. Then she said look at the flower for 20 minutes, that should give you 10 minutes to paint it. She handed me the bag of paints and started opening the door. But I began talking and I told her about Thursday. She said she wanted to talk with me about it, to come back at 10:30.

So, with my bag of paints and my yellow daffodil, I headed toward the Experimental Psychology Laboratory. There

I sat and I looked
So this might be called thoughts

While looking at a daffodil.
I thought how little the names
I had learned in biology had to do
What what a flower is, stamen,
Pistil, and all the parts, what is
Important is the whole, the flower
And its beauty—the feeling emitted to
People. I wanted to be small enough to
Step inside the horn of the daffodil and
Follow the tunnel, to be engulfed by its
Power, its beauty, its existence. How like
Crepe paper the rim of the horn is, how can
Nature crinkle its products in such a delightful way.

Then I thought I must look at its form,
Its structure, if I am to know how to draw it.
I looked, I saw the texture, the strength and
Yet the fragility, the softness and yet the
Roughness. I saw the delicate petals, their points
Reaching out. I saw that they were not formed in
Perfect evenness, but nature formed them in a
Pleasing informal unevenness. Because the flower was
Not quite open, I tenderly opened the petals to
Their extension. So before me a full mature flower,
But somehow I thought of it as a baby,
Proud on its green stem, but it did not know
That it was going to die, in fact,
It was already dead.

And now to paint, I wet the paper and applied yellow paint. I can never get over the surge of pleasure I feel when I place my left hand into the paint and begin to move and manipulate the wet paint into some rhythm, grace, pattern. I could not get a front view of the daffodil, so I attempted a profile. Somewhere along the line, I decided that flowers have rhythm and if I could paint I would not portray them with realistic, structure forms, but as a rhythm and feeling presented by that particular flower. So I placed a full horn (trumpet) and swirled around it the petals. Again I was not pleased with the results. I attempted several. The pleasure I felt was one of having experienced something that had meaning for me.

The bell rang and I hurriedly cleaned up in order to get back and talk to Dr. Fagan. I said I brought your flower back. She said it's opening right up. I said I think I helped it some. Then a brief moment of uncomfortableness on my part, not knowing what to do. She said sit down (her chair was back). So I picked up the bag of paints I had placed there and plopped my pocketbook on the floor and sat down. I for some reason can't remember what I said—oh, yes, I began by saying I felt I had a greater capacity for feelings than most people, a greater range and intensity. I continued that for some reason the music had disturbed me, I felt shaken, couldn't cope with it. She said anything that bothered me I didn't have to do, I could stop. I said no that's not what I want to do. I want to know why? Why on that day with that music, what happened? Why should being in a room with a tape recorder bring such an intense emotional response from me? Other sessions had been intense, but I could handle them and had often been elated—(she said earlier in the conversation that I should have talked with her on Thursday). But I couldn't handle Thursday. She said she felt the need for feedback and suggested I come back and talk a few minutes each time, even though there was so little time. I said well I'm not sure that will do much good because that's me. I can talk about Thursday on Monday and Monday on Thursday but not Monday on Monday. Sometime in the conversation she said she needed to know if I were still in treatment, wouldn't want to interfere with that. I said no, I had quit last May.

I can't remember the exact words, I talked about the fact that almost missing the session might have made me more sensitive than usual. The bell rang and I left because we were both late for class.

February 16

Yesterday after or while writing I began to see some answers to why Thursday had been so intense. First I began to analyze the music that I had listened to. The first music was the two selections each with its own circle of emotions, although each was at a different end of the continuum, not intermixed. So I could listen with one set of feelings and then switch after the pause to another set of feelings opposite from the first. The second music had only one change, this from a powerful to a soft interlude. But the music I heard Thursday was varied—the patterns, the type, the extremes—produced in me a variability of emotions, like therapy in a capsule (or nutshell), like every emotion I had ever felt all togther, like I was an instrument and every note had been played upon me in every possible combination.

Now this explains why that particular music hit me so. But there is more, I was predisposed to question how meaningful the situation should be, how foolish I can feel about some situations, how vulnerable I feel. I may have written this before but I will write it again to work through it. I knew Monday that Dr. Fagan might be out of town on Friday. On Monday I had wanted to ask if she would be out of town Friday and if so could I come on another day, but I didn't get to ask. On Wednesday, when she told me, I felt unhappy although I should have been glad because I had an Experimental Psychology test and could use that extra study time. Somehow I still felt foolish not being able to miss a session. During the next class I was painfully aware that missing was going to bother me. That's when I went by and asked Dr. Fagan if I could come Thursday. So the music reinforced my feelings of why things mean so much to me, why I feel foolish that they do, and why I feel so vulnerable.

February 16

I decided last night that I wanted to tell Dr. Fagan the answers I had come up with and that I felt better about it now. I told her I had come up with some answers about Thursday, would she like to hear them? She said yes and to sit down. She moved some books from the chair and I sat down. I did not experience the usual uncomfortable feeling that I have when I attempt to communicate with someone, particularly someone who means something to me. I began with my analysis about the music and then continued through the feelings of desertion and vulnerability. Then I said I felt better and hopped up and started to leave.

She said hold on, she wanted to have her say. So I sat back down. I can't remember how she started but she did say something like—there is more going on here than she knew about or was getting told about. I said I was worried about taking up too much of her time. She was angry, she said for me not to be hostile, let *her* handle her time. She said something about wanting the communications to come from me. She said if I couldn't talk, then she would suggest I write, but I had already said I was doing that. Yes, I said, I asked if she wanted to read it? She said whatever I wanted. I said I had planned to type it and give it to her at the end of the quarter. She said it was up to me. I said I wanted her to read it now, if she didn't mind the writing, etc. I was pleased to be able to give it to her. I opened my notebook and took it out (all on notebook paper) and said you will notice one effect of what you have done for me is more quantity of words. She took the papers and placed them on her desk. I said one other thing I wanted to say was that on an Experimental Psychology test I had gotten all the points on the essay questions, although I had not done well on the test as a whole. My husband and I noticed a significant improvement in endings, spelling, and ability to express myself.

February 17

I began by saying I was sorry that I had not talked with her about what I was experiencing, because she could have no way of knowing how I felt without my telling her. She sure couldn't judge from my behavior. And I felt sorry for all the people I hadn't talked to, particularly my husband.

I can't recall all she said or how she said it. She began by saying that reading the diary had been a moving experience for her. She listed some underlying trends running through it and at the time they all seemed so clear and now I can't remember them. (My not believing I had a right to feelings. Rejection, do I have to go ahead with my response and accept what follows.) I said that I can't believe anyone would see me as worth helping. That my enthusiasm has to be controlled. I drive people away with my enthusiasm. She said so you know what you are calling me? I said no. She said think about it. I did (with bowed head) but couldn't think. So she said I'll give you a few adjectives bored, deceived, etc. You are saying that I am the kind of person who can be bored by you, etc. She counted the adjectives and then the phrases on her fingers. I can't remember the exact words, but she was saying that my low self-concept was calling her names. She asked if I thought that was nice. No I said. She said I think it's pretty nasty (mean).

Silence (when I was so thankful she didn't say can't you tell me about what you are thinking, or something similar).

I began again, I am afraid to talk and expose myself for fear of getting hurt. I used to say if I ever became psychotic, I would be catatonic. Then I would not be hurt any more.

She said more to me, prison, power, little details messed up, picking people in my life, behavior, response. She said that I felt everyone else was born knowing how to behave. No one perfect, everyone has a bellybutton. Power, I always felt that if I really released myself on the world, it just could not take it.

So she told me about the misconcepts I had of myself and the world. Somehow all of it was rather nice, painful but nice, because they were all things about me that I would rather not have affirmed. When she finished talking, she said she would like to read me some poems. I was amazed. She read several from one book and then from another. I asked if I could borrow the book, she said yes. She picked up another book, but I have some more to read. Then she said no you can't borrow them, but I will reread any that you want.

February 18

I had so much to say today. I felt that I had 100,000,000 things to say and there will never be enough time to do so. I went by her office but the bell had already rung and I met her coming out of the door. She said did you want to see me? I said well I think I'm late. We started walking down the stairs. I said I just wanted her to know that I had a pretty exciting afternoon. I showed the book I had gotten and I was pleased with it. She said that's not the best one, Alan Watts is better. We parted, but I wanted to talk. I felt frustrated by not knowing what to do. I felt that I had learned a thousand new concepts about myself and life in the past three days. I wanted to tell her about yesterday, that after leaving her I had gone by the library and selected three books, one on Zen, one on loneliness, and one on the need to love. Then I walked out with Margaret—into the rain. I told Margaret let's walk through the park and I stepped in puddles and held my mouth up to taste the rain. It was like I had been in the hospital for months, years, and suddenly I could step back into the world and once again perceive all the wonders that I had almost forgotten existed.

All afternoon I either read Zen or thought about our talk. I was in a state of complete wonderment. Like I wanted to go saying wow, wow, wow! Like the poem. I felt like a hen who had suddenly been transformed into a sea gull and someone had said fly and I flew. Or rather like (after reading Zen and feeling that some of my own ideas were unfolding before my eyes in a more sensible form) I had been a sea gull all the time but thought I was a chicken. Now Dr. Fagan says YOU ARE A SEA GULL and I know that I am. But best of all is that way up there are a thousand other sea gulls for me to soar with. I am not alone.

February 19

So the sea gull swooped into Georgia State via her old Chevrolet, unloaded some frames and raced to see if there really are other sea gulls and if she were really a sea gull. But, alas, she was still a chicken.

I stood in the hall. She opened her office door and went in. She opened the other door and then went back to hers. I walked over to her door and stood on the outside looking in. She thought a moment and reached for three sheets of paper. I followed her into the other office. She said write three criticisms I have of other people and then five of myself, and write big.

And I was furious, I was so mad. I wanted to talk and she put me in there to write. I wrote large and I was so mad that I looked up the words I couldn't spell. Twice the phone rang and I answered it. I kept writing and getting madder and madder. I wanted to stop and go turn in the paper, but I couldn't. I thought maybe if I fill up all the paper I can go turn it in. But I sat there. NO BELL. Dr. Fagan knocked on the door and said that it was almost time for class—they're not ringing bells today. I said, oh, they aren't.

So I folded up my mad paper, picked up my books, and walked over to give the paper to her and turned to go. She said something—wait a minute or something and I turned back. She put my paper into the file and brought out the papers which I had written my diary on. I took them and she handed me a book and said, "This may clear up some things for you." I took it and left. I don't think I said thank you, but may have. I went over to use the calculator and I sat in that little room and closed the door. And I said I am so damn mad I can't go to class. I will go and see her after class and I hope she has read my paper. I sat and read the book she had given me (*Psychotherapy East and West*) which I had ordered in the bookstore yesterday out of a list of ten of Watt's books.

I stomped up to her office and waited. She arrived and we went in. I said "Did you read what I wrote?" She said No, I never read it unless you tell (or want) me to. I sad "Well read it." She reached up and took it out of her file and read it. My anger blared out in every word. I had written the criticisms as I was told. She finished reading. She asked "What do you do with your anger?"

"I don't know." I said I appreciated her not saying during my silences—can't you tell me about or something soapy like that. I struggled to think and to answer her.

A.: I am angry at you and at me.
F.: Why are you angry at me?
A.: I think because you told me to write and should have known that I needed to talk.
F.: What else, are you disappointed with me?
A.: Yes, I thought you should have known better.
F.: Why are you angry at yourself?
A.: Because I did not say anything about it, because I did what I was told, because I sat in there and wrote when I wanted to come out.
F.: How are you going to punish yourself?

Criticism

I dont want to write any damn criticism I want to talk to you, I have 100,000,000 things to say and there will never be enough time to say it in.

Criticism of other people

They are narrow minded, stupid, and unflexiable. They won't listen to me or attempt to understand what I am saying. If they appear to understand they start off with "I understand, but" and then they let you know they didn't understand at all.

They will not take the time to look around at all the lovely things in life. If you do and if you appreciate these, they can't understand -- they look at you like you're crazy. And they misinterpretate like to such an extent that they don't even know where the beauty lies.

What I hate most about me

I hate not being able to let someone know when I need them -- the hardest thing in the world is to admit you need someone and the second hardest is to tell them about it and when I need someone I want to say please don't leave me and I can't,

When I experience something it hits me so completely that it engulfs my whole life. I can't make it go away or handle in a nonchalant manner. I think and think and think and can't turn it off.

I can't respond angrily when I want to. I can be mad as hell and I won't do anything about it, I just smolder. It takes me awhile to incorporate new ideas and concepts into myself. I can't just hear it once, I have to hear it over and over and over. I have to feel complete wonderment and awe, I have to rehash each new idea a million times. I wish I could hear something once and have it and not to be so stupid. I feel foolish so much of the time and I hate it. I don't know what to do about it. In fact I don't really know what to do about a lot of things.

I want to be brilliant and I just can't quite manage it. I run and I run and I run and I keep saying I am not going to run any more and I do.

I get so completely absorbed in what I am doing that I can't analysis it until much later, all of me is experiencing there is nothing left wh with which to analysis or make judgements.

I feel humble and I don't want to go around feeling humble. I want to demand and have a right to demand and have my demands responded to. (I keep ending sentences in prep.)

Right now I could knock a whole in the wall or ~~exployed explered~~ explode -- (when I am mad with a word I can't ~~sle~~ spell it) and I won't do anything about it. I'll just sit here and write.

If I have power over people I have not been aware of it. I want the power but I want to recognize it and use it appropriately.

Words that I hate right now -- power, control, conform, good, sweet behave, details, anxiety, explode, anger, fear, need, humble, foolish, embarrass, complement, vulnerable, intense, baby, crying.

Fig. 4. Anne's Criticisms of Other People and Herself

A.: Well, I didn't go to class, I guess that's a punishment, otherwise I don't know.

F.: So, you're calling yourself names. [How nervous I was, I kept flipping the pages of my book.]

She held out her hand, palm up and told me to put my hand against it. I said "Why?" She said go ahead and do it. So I put my hand up to hers. She pushed and I pushed—rather like Indian wrestling, but she would ease up at times and never really pushed hard. She took her hand away and I put mine down.

F.: What did you feel?

A.: Pressure.

F.: Go on, what else? [*Pause.*] What else? [She was smiling but I could not continue.]
OK. I'll tell you what hopefully you felt. That when I meet you halfway, no one wins, no one loses. I hoped you were aware of your arm, your shoulder because awareness of self comes from pushing against someone else. [And she said something I can't remember which I asked her to repeat.] OK, let's put it another way. You are more afraid of your fears than I am. [*Pause.*]

A.: OK, what am I afraid of? [*Pause.*] Am I afraid of me, or anger, or you?

F.: That's not a question that gets answered right away. [I knew it was time to go and began picking up my things. She looked at my paper again.] I am glad to see this firm writing.

A.: And big.

F.: Yes, you are big and John Hancock said he wrote his name big so the king wouldn't need his spectacles.

I said thank you and left.

Friday while sitting in the car at the Y, a poem came to me, I took a piece of cardboard and jotted it down. When I came home I wrote it out, and corrected a few prepositions to keep the rhythm smooth.

I was pleased with the poem. All through my personal belongings are snatches of paper with poems on them. Only none of the poems are any good—they are good ideas poorly executed. They are jerky and lack rhythm. But this poem flowed smoothly (or so I thought) and it expressed exactly what I wanted it to say. I was delighted. I really felt like a sea gull, or like a sea gull who had thought she was a chicken and never knew the difference until another sea gull told her how to fly. And I flew. All weekend I soared and swooped and glided so filled with feelings and ideas and thoughts and freedom. I felt like a jet plane mind in a Model T body. I felt like I had been around the world several times in the past few days.

Anyway. I was in seventh heaven, I had communicated, I was growing, I was reading Alan Watts. I was happy, busy, and up on my schoolwork, looking forward to having more time to read on my own.

NOW IN THE MIDDLE OF THIS ROSY PICTURE ALL HELL BROKE LOOSE.

(On February 23rd a crisis arose for Anne that occupied all her time outside the basic requirements of family and courses. The experiment as such had to be discontinued, and in essence ends here. Anne's diary describes this problem, the difficulties involved, and her surprise and pleasure when in spite of her fears and self-doubts she was able to cope with it successfully.)

March 17

I have not written anything in this diary since February 19. The events which have occurred will explain why. But before I try to catch up, I have to write about today. I went up to say goodby to Dr. Fagan.

F.: Would you like the tape you listened to?
A.: Yes.
F.: What do you want to do with your materials?
A.: I don't know.

There was a woman at the door with a little boy, who needed her card signed. While Dr. Fagan signed it I tried to think what she meant by the question and what I should answer.

A.: I think I would like to take them with me.
F.: OK.

She went back to her office and handed me the manila folder and the tape. I was rather puzzled, a little confused. I didn't know if she only meant for me to listen to it (which I had wanted to do again since the first hearing) or whether she was giving it to me. I asked. She said, "You may have it if you want." When she offered me the tape, I knew she understood how much the whole thing had meant to me and she knew I would want to keep it. I still did not know what to think about her asking about the materials. After thinking about it I decided she asked me to see what I would do. And that I had taken them because I felt that I could not go back to the stages of finger-painting, free-association writing, and writing what I heard to music. I wanted to continue, I hated to think it had passed, and yet I had the feeling more exciting adventures lay waiting for me to discover in light of my past experiences.

I wondered if somehow Dr. Fagan feels this also, that I have gained a great deal from what has happened, but am ready to go on to something else.

Can this be the end? Is it all here in this manila folder? I can't believe it. I walked away aware of every pressure of my feet on the stairs, aware of the bent folder and its contents, aware of every sensation I was feeling. I opened the door and walked out. The wind blew my hair. I felt the wind on my face and the hair blowing around it. I smelled rain in the air.

chapter 8

DREAM SEMINARS*

Frederick S. Perls

I

Freud once called the dream "the royal road to the unconscious." I believe that it is really the royal road to *integration.* I never know what the unconscious is, but we know that the dream is definitely the most spontaneous production we have. It comes about with our intention, work, or deliberation. If you want to understand what you do with the dream, there is no better way than the way I will show you.

If you want to work on your own dreams, do it together with somebody else, because, as I will try to point out, around the sick point you will get phobic. You will try to avoid—run away—suddenly get sleepy, or have something very important to do. If you have a partner to work with, he can see this phobic attitude. Generally, the neurotic only fools himself—he only thinks he fools other people.

Now I'd like to do a little bit of systematic work. Dreamwork can be fun. Actually it's very sincere work. You will notice those who work on dreams the way I suggest—namely, *without interpretations, with-*

* Transcribed from workshops held at Esalen Institute, 1966.

out interference by your computer, the thinker—derive a great benefit from it.

Before I go further in theory, I would like somebody to come up here with me. I had two offers—one from Mary Anne, who has worked with me before and is willing to come up and work on a dream.

Now, we do the dream. To be systematic, we do it in several stages. We want to bring the dream back to life. First the patient tells her dream like a story—something that happened to her.

Mary Anne's Dream

M. A.: My dream—the first part of the dream—I was sitting, looking, watching, off to the side of the shore. There were some rather fat naked women, and I could only see their backs.

Then the next part of the dream that I remember, I was on a promontory overlooking the ocean. It was a very steep cliff—down. And a cow came out of the water with horns, with a little calf beside her. And there was a man dressed in white. He reminded me of my father. And he yelled—I don't remember what he said. But, whatever he yelled—there was a man over here—and a man over here, also dressed in white—with megaphones. And, they did something. And so all these cows that were starting to come out of the water with their calves went back. And there were a lot of . . . then some other people came along. They were sort of . . . and they—why doesn't he let them come? It's time for them to come, and I felt it was time for them to come. Why doesn't he make them come? And he said something about the shore. He didn't want to let them come. It wasn't time. So I decided to go in swimming. And so I asked him if it would disturb the cows if I went in swimming. And he said no.

So, I took off my shift and went in swimming. And as I was swimming, something grabbed my hand—a jaw. And then something grabbed my other hand. It didn't bite it though, but it just held it firmly. And I don't know how I got back out of the water. I think I got my left hand free—got back out of the water. And on my right hand was a little Pekinese dog, sort of a bedraggled one. He was a cow-herding dog. And he let loose. He didn't hurt my hand. That was the end of the dream.

PERLS: There's so much material in this dream—can you pick up a little part of the dream, and say it again in the *present tense:* as if you were dreaming it *now?*

M. A.: I like the part about the cows coming out of the water. I see the cows. First, I see the cow coming out of the water with her calf. And then I see the man, making the other men sending the cows back. I see all these cows in the water with their noses up, like water buffaloes sniffing when they come up for air. Then they sink down.

PERLS: Do you actually see them now? Or do you just say so?

M. A.: I remember.

PERLS: But you don't see them.

M. A.: No.

PERLS: Could you tell the same thing again and try to *see.*

M. A.: I see the cow coming out of the water with her calf. And I see the man yelling to the other man. And the cow goes *back* in the water, and all the cows *stay.* I see them snuffing around.

PERLS: Did you see it this time? Now can you set the scene? You're now the stage director. Where is the ocean? Where are the cows? You begin to psychodramatize—

M. A.: The ocean's out there. All these people are the cows. And they're all under water, sniffing. And there's a little bit of shore between the ocean and the cliff. I'm on top of the cliff. And I'm very resentful that this man doesn't let the cows come out.

PERLS: Now, let's start acting it out. Tell this to the man. Talk to the man—express your resentment.

M. A.: I want those cows to come out! You have no business telling those other men to yell with their megaphones for the cows to stay back in. And I don't see how you can get cows to stay in the water by yelling at them, anyway.

PERLS: What does he answer?

M. A.: He answers, "But *I* am the person who knows about cows. I know when they come out, and when they shouldn't come out. And I can control those men with the megaphones. And I have some magic noises that the cows respond to—that keep them in the water. And I know best."

PERLS: Now, play this role again, and tell this to the audience.

M. A.: I know best about those cows. I have some kind of inner vision, and I know that they shouldn't come out of the water at this time. They don't belong here right now. I don't want them here. I tell these other . . . I don't have to even bother doing it myself. I tell these other men to keep them back—and they stay back.

PERLS: Now, say this to the cows.

M. A.: Stay back cows . . . Oh-h—I don't want them to stay back. I want them to come.

PERLS: You have to fight for control.

M. A.: Yes.

PERLS: Now, go on. Have it out with them. Let's see who wins.

M. A.: You have that secret message, and the know-how. And I partly feel that you know what you're doing, but partly feel that *I want* those cows to come out—now. And all these other people over here want them to come out now. So, you tell them to come out. I don't sound very convincing.

PERLS: Who says that?

M. A.: Me. You see, I really think he probably knows what he's doing.

PERLS: Can you say this to me?

M. A.: Do you know what you're doing? Part of the time, you do.

PERLS: Well, I don't see any integration yet between you and this man. You're still at loggerheads.

M. A.: I am the man [*pounding*]. And those cows do what I say! And I don't give a—

PERLS: Who are you hitting?

M. A.: [*Pounding*] You!

PERLS: You are hitting me?

M. A.: I don't know.

PERLS: Is he hitting Mary Anne?

M. A.: Yes, he's hitting me.

PERLS: How do you feel when he is hitting you?

M. A.: . . . Oh, God!

PERLS: You feel, oh, God?

M. A.: Um-hum.

PERLS: When he is hitting you, you suddenly become religious. Does this mean anything to you?

M. A.: God?

PERLS: Yes. When you are being hit, you discover God?

M. A.: No.

PERLS: But is he God, by any chance?

M. A.: I don't know. Yeah, I feel . . . I suppose so, he's God. He's an all-powerful hitter!

PERLS: So, God is a hitter?

M. A.: Yeah [*pounding*]! And he has a hell of a good time!

PERLS: All right now. You be God and hit with vengeance.

M. A.: [*Pounding*] I hate people that don't want cows to come out! Sit down, cows! Sit down, nice cows. I encompass everything.

PERLS: OK. I think you have gained a bit of strength. Now I want you to play the cows. I think you have to go over there.

M. A.: With all these other cows? I'm the cow that comes out of the water first, sneaks up the shore . . . I am the cow—with horns. And I've got a little calf. I think the little calf has horns, too. We come up around the edge of the promontory. We're very happy about coming out. It's great to be out of the water. And here's this horn yelling at us. And, my God, why should we pay any attention to a horn! So we—

PERLS: You are the cow. Talk to him. You are a happy cow.

M. A.: Yeah, coming out of the water. "And, listen. You're so damn high up there [*raising her voice*]. You're telling *me* to go back in the water? I'll stay right up here!" And then I go up and kick him.

PERLS: Now, change roles. Become God again.

M. A.: Listen, you cow. I don't give a shit, if you kick me. I've been kicked before. And I've got this big horn. And I know, God damn well, that you're going to go back when I blow it.

PERLS: How does the cow respond?

M. A.: That cow's kind of beaten down. The cow says, "I don't dare—I don't dare gore you like I want to do!"

PERLS: Oh-h. Say this again.

M. A.: I don't dare gore you like I want to.

PERLS: Say it again.

M. A.: I don't dare *gore* you like I *want* to! [*Pause*] But I *want* to!

PERLS: Now, the power part is wanting to open again.

M. A.: Yeah. The cow is standing there. The cow doesn't see what this horn has to do with it—you know—if that man is up there pushing with pitchforks, that would be all right. But this horn—

PERLS: What role are you playing? *Be* the cow.

M. A.: I don't understand why this horn just paralyzes me. *Your* horn paralyzes me—I am *paralyzed* by that horn!

PERLS: He has a horn?

M. A.: He's got . . . well, that man over there is talking to this man who has the horn.

PERLS: But the cows also have horns.

M. A.: Yeah. *I* have horns, *too!* I could go right in your horn and gore your mouth out. But I am going to stand here in the sand and not move back, anyway. And you can sit up there with your horn, and toot—and I'm *still* paralyzed, but I *won't* go back!

PERLS: Say this again.

M. A.: I *won't go* back!

PERLS: Louder.

M. A.: I *won't go* back!

PERLS: What does he say now?

M. A.: He says . . . "My God" . . . he says, "if . . . This horn isn't that effective." He says, "To Hell with it." He throws it away.

PERLS: So the under-dog wins again. What do you feel now?

M. A.: Oh, I don't know. I feel kind of . . . just depleted. I'm wondering if this cow is really—has the strength to stay there, or if she's just pretending to herself, or if—if she's just defiant for nothing at all. This horn is just *nothing*. All this defiance and this turning back is just for nothing, you know, just for nothing. And yet, all this time . . . with the energy wasted. She could go out there with her calf and have her grass and her water. And she just sits there in the sand. That's better to be there than in the water.

PERLS: Let's find out. Go back to the water and play the water. What kind of water is this? The ocean?

M. A.: Yes, it's the ocean. It's calm—

PERLS: Play the ocean, *I* am . . .

M. A.: I am the ocean. And I, sort of, surround all these cows. And I've nurtured them, and I love them and here, they want to go away.

PERLS: Talk to them.

M. A.: Here, you all cows, I try to let you become alive and live in this ocean, that I am, and I surround you, and you have your calves, and I don't see why you're not happy. So, why don't you just stay here. It's pleasant. You can come up for air —You've got somebody up there on the shore telling you what to do—it's safe. Just stay here, cows, and be with me. Let me, sort of, lap around you. We'll have a pleasant time.

PERLS: What do the cows ask?

M. A.: Oh, the cows say, "*God, no!* We're restless and unhappy in this ocean. We want *more* air than just a sniff, and—than just a sniff now and then. We want to have grass and clear water. We want to live. So we're going to leave you."

PERLS: Now, which parts of the dream can you really identify as being *yourself?*

M. A.: I'm the cow, and I'm the man that's keeping them back, and I'm the onlooker, and I'm the little dog that bites my hand—I don't know about the ocean. The more I think about this ocean, the more insidious it gets—and the more it's like saying, "stay with me and I'll give you honey forever—a little LSD, and peace and quiet, and you'll be happy."

PERLS: You're not mistaken, the ocean represents safety?

M. A.: I guess so, yeah.

PERLS: Protection

M. A.: Yeah. And it's knowing where you are. I can't identify—

PERLS: You can't identify? Say this to the ocean.

M. A.: I'm sorry, ocean. I just don't dig you. I don't feel that I'm you. I feel that you *engulf* me—I want to get rid of you, this waving ocean, all that you do to me—the salt water that gets in my nose. And yet, this ocean is—kind of loving, and nice, and slippery, and—I don't know if *I* am loving, slippery—Maybe I could be the ocean.

PERLS: Yeah?

M. A.: I am the ocean. I am loving and slipping over you cows, and there's some seaweed that's around, that you can eat. And some sea otters to give you a little entertainment. And, I *am* the ocean, because the ocean—I am everything being the ocean. I cover—but I know I don't really, because I know there's that land up there, and there's that man with the horn—I guess that the real problem is the man and the ocean.

PERLS: The ocean representing what, and the man representing what?

M. A.: I don't know. The man, I—sort of, think of as my father—a controlling, repellent force that I *want* to go to, and yet I don't want to go to. And the ocean, I think. I . . . it's awfully hard for me to feel for this ocean. I don't know what this ocean is—what *you* are, ocean. I don't know what you are. But, partly, you're going to suffocate me, and I think that this ocean is *much* harder for me to deal with than this man. Then I think, well—

the ocean is my mother, but then—maybe, this is true, though. Maybe this ocean is—very slippery and—

PERLS: You know, I don't like to interpret, but to me, this is so obvious that I think I will interfere here. To me, it seems the ocean represents your female part, and the other is the male part. It's the female —the *caring, loving* part—and the other is the fighting, domineering, controlling part of you. So, I think you are right when you say those are the two antagonists. So could you have an encounter with these two parts of you?

M. A.: Well, it's a million times easier. The man part: As the man, I boss people around—keep things back, and I've got my feet on the ground, and . . . It's the woman—this is very hard.

PERLS: I want you to just let the man go into the ocean and see what happens.

M. A.: I, the man, go into the ocean?

PERLS: Yes, you as the man.

M. A.: Well, I—as the man, I won't have anything to do with that ocean. But, if you tell me to go in—

PERLS: Yeah. I'm interested in how this man would control the ocean. He can control cows, apparently.

M. A.: I take off my clothes, and I go into the ocean. And I'd just be a little tiny, itty-bitty speck swimming around in that ocean, with all those cows and all that seaweed. I wouldn't amount to a hill of beans, so I'd have to come right out!

PERLS: What would happen if the ocean came to the man?

M. A.: Then the ocean would lose her identity, because she'd have to come up onto the land, and she wouldn't be an ocean anymore—she'd be a little stream. And, I, as the ocean—I don't want to be a little stream. I want to be an ocean. And I, as the ocean, *resent* that man. He's *different* from me. *He stands up,* and *I* spread out. And I don't like anything different.

PERLS: Say this again.

M. A.: I don't like anything different from me. I want to be it all.

PERLS: So, be it all! Be the ocean, and be the man. This is the essence. Instead of having a conflict—either/or—the male or the female—be both. This has been known for ages, that the conflict between the male and female cycle in a person produces neurosis. Integration produces the genius. All geniuses have *both* male *and* female aspects. The really mature person is ambidextrous. He not only uses both hands, he reacts both emotionally and aggressively toward the world.

Well, I think you can now do some more work on your own. Thank you.

You see, we've demonstrated that all the different parts, *any* part in the dream—is yourself, is a projection of yourself. If there are inconsistent sides, contradictory sides, and you use them up to fight each other, you come again to the eternal *inner conflict game.* You find in all these encounters that the two parties are usually hostile at first. But if we work long enough, then you come through to an understanding and . . . an appreciation of differences.

We couldn't get to the point, yet, where Mary Anne could *appreciate* the difference. An ocean is *not* a he-man, and a he-man is not an ocean. But, both have potentials which might be useful and valuable by themselves.

So, since all impoverishment of the personality comes about by self-alienation—by disowning parts of ourselves, either by repression or by projection—the remedy is, of course, *re-identification*. We achieve the identification by *playing* the parts of the dream. We *become* the part until we begin to recognize it as a bit of ourselves—and then it becomes our own again. Then, we begin to grow and gain in potential and maturation.

The psychoanalytical approach to a dream is to make it an intellectual game by interpretations and fixed pseudosymbolic statements: this is sexual, the horn is a phallus symbol, the cow is the mother symbol. But we don't get very far by interpretation.

All right, who would like to work on a dream now?

Carol's Dream

C.: I dreamed that I saw a lake drying up. There's a small island in the middle of the lake and a circle of, well, porpoises. They're like porpoises except they can stand up, so, they're like porpoises that are like people. They're in a circle—sort of like a religious ceremony—and it's very sad. I feel very sad, because . . . they can breathe—they are sort of dancing around in a circle—but the water, their element, is drying up. So, it's like a dying—like watching a race of people or a race of creatures dying. And they're mostly females, but a few of them have a small male organ so there are a few males there. But they won't live long enough to reproduce—and their element is drying up. One is sitting over here near me. I'm talking to him, and he has prickles on his tummy—sort of—like a porcupine. They don't seem to be a part of him. And, I think there's one good point about the water drying up. I think—well, at least at the bottom, when all the water dries up, there will probably be some sort of treasure there, because at the bottom of the lake there should be things that have fallen, like coins or something like that. I look carefully, and all I can find is an old license plate. That's the dream.

PERLS: Will you please play this license plate.

C.: I am an old license plate, thrown in the bottom of a lake. I have no use because I'm of no value. I'm not rusted, I'm outdated. So, I can't be used. I'm just thrown on the rubbish heap. That's what I did with the license plate—I threw it in the rubbish heap.

PERLS: Well, what do you feel about the dream?

C.: I don't like it. I don't like being an old license plate—useless.

PERLS: Could you talk about it until you come to be the license plate.

C.: Useless—outdated. The use of the license plate is to allow—to give a car permission to go—and I can't give anyone permission to do anything because I'm outdated. In California they just paste a little—you buy a sticker and stick it on the car—on the old license plates. So, maybe someone would put me on their car and stick a new sticker on me. I don't . . .

PERLS: OK. Play now the lake.

C.: I am a lake. I am drying up and disappearing—soaking into the earth—*dying*. But, when I soak into the earth and become part of the earth maybe, I water the surrounding area, so—even the lake—even in my bed—flowers can grow. New, like can grow [*starting to cry*] from me—

PERLS: Do you get the existential message?

C.: Yes, I can—I can create. I can create beauty—I can no longer reproduce. I'm like the porpoise—I'm . . . But, I—I keep wanting to say, "food." I—as water, become—I *water* the earth and give life—growing things. The water—they need both the earth and the water—and the air and sun. But, as the water and the lake, I can play a part.

PERLS: You see the contrast—on the surface you find some *thing,* some artifact—the license plate—the artificial you. But, when you go deeper, you find the apparent *death* of the lake is actually fertility.

C.: I don't really like this plate—or permission—or a license plate in order to—

PERLS: Nature doesn't need a license plate to grow. You don't have to be useless if you are organically creative—and you just found that you are. Thank you.

JEAN'S DREAM

J.: This was a long time ago. I'm not sure how it started. I think it, sort of, started in the—the New York subway—and kind of, paying—putting a token in and going through the turnstile, and walking a little ways down the corridors and then, kind of, turning a corner. And I realized that somewhere or another in here—instead of being a subway, it seemed like—there was, sort of like —inclines that started going down into the earth.

Somewhere or another at just about this point, as I discovered this incline, my mother was with me. Or, well, maybe she was when I started—I can't remember. At any rate, there was this incline. It was sort—of muddy; sort—of slippery. And I thought, "Oh, we can go down this!" On the side or somewhere, I picked up a leftover carton. It was flattened out, or maybe I flattened it out. At any rate, I said, "Let's sit down on this." And I sat down on the edge and kind of made a toboggan out of it. And I said, "Mom, you sit down behind me," and we started going down. And it sort of went around—and there were other people—it seemed like, waiting in line. But then they kind of disappeared.

Anyway, we were just going down and around. And it was—it just kept going down and down and down—and I was sort of realizing—I was going down into the bowels of the earth. And every once in awhile, I'd turn around and say, "Fun?" Maybe I was a little scared, but it seemed like it was fun. Yet I wondered what would be found at the bottom of this.

Then, finally, it leveled out. And we got up, and I was just astounded! Because here I thought, "Oh, my God—this is the bowels of the earth." And yet, instead of being dark—it was like there was sunlight coming from somewhere—and this beautiful—oh—I've never been to Florida, but it seemed like Florida—everglades, with lagoons and things like that. And I don't remember *saying* anything particular except—maybe something like, "Who would have ever expected this?"

Now, when the dreamer tells a story like this, you take it just as a single incident, or an unfinished situation, or wish fulfillment. But, if he tells it in the present —as *mirroring* his existence—it immediately has a different aspect. It's not just an occasional happening.

We think of dreams as *night* dreams. But, what we don't realize enough, is that we devote our lives to dreams—of glory, usefulness, being a do-gooder, or whatever we dream of. For many people, through self-frustration, the dream turns into a nightmare. The task of *all* deep religions, especally Zen Buddhism, or of good therapy, is the Great Awakening—the coming *to one's senses*—waking up from one's dream, especially from one's nightmare.

We start to see, to feel, to experience our needs, to find satisfaction instead of playing the roles and needing such a lot of props—houses, motor cars, dozens and dozens of costumes. We burden ourselves with millions of unnecessary ballasts, not realizing that all property is given to us only for the duration, anyhow. We can't take it with us.

This idea of *waking up* and becoming real—of existing with what we have—the real full potential—the rich life, deep experiences, joy, anger, being *real*—not zombies . . . that's the meaning of *real* therapy—of real maturation—of *real* waking up—instead of this permanent self-deception and fantasizing, seeking impossible goals, feeling sorry for ourselves that we can't play the part we want to play, and so, on and on.

Well, let's return to our lady.

PERLS: So, Jean, could you tell again, the dream? Live it through, as if it were your existence, and see whether you can understand more about your life.

J.: Well, I know it doesn't really seem clear until I find myself—the place has become, kind of—top of the shoot. I don't remember whether at first I was afraid or not, possibly. Oh, I shouldn't say this now—I mean. I guess I'm—

PERLS: Are you afraid to go down?

J.: I guess I'm a little afraid to go down. But then it seems like—

PERLS: But you have to go down.

J.: I guess I'm afraid to find out what's there.

PERLS: Does it point to a false ambition—that you are too high up?

J.: That's true.

PERLS: So the existentialists say, "Go down—it's fun." Of course, again our mentality says, "High up, is better than down." We always want to go somewhere *higher than.*

J.: Anyway, I seem a little afraid to go down.

PERLS: Talk to the chute.

J.: Why are you muddy? You're slippery and slidey, and I might fall on you and slip.

PERLS: Now, play the chute. "I'm slippery and muddy . . ."

J.: I'm slippery and muddy—the better to slide, and the faster to get down. (*Laughter*)

PERLS: Well, now, what's the joke?

J.: I'm slippery! (*With laughter*)

PERLS: Can you accept yourself as slippery?

J.: I guess so. Yes, I can never seem to—you know—always just when I think I'm about to—you know, say, "Aha. I caught you now," it slips away—rationalization. I'm slippery and slidey. Hm-m-m.

Anyway, I'm going to go down, because it looks like it would be fun. And I want to find out where it goes and what's going to be at the end. And it seems perhaps—only now . . . I . . . in turning around and looking to see what I could use—to protect my britches, or maybe make a better slide—I discover this cardboard.

PERLS: Can you play this cardboard? What's your function?

J.: I'm just to make things easier. I'm just kind of lying around there—almost left over—but, aha, I have a use for—I can be useful. And I'm not just left over and lying around—and we can make it easier to get down.

PERLS: Is it important for you to be useful?

J.: Yes. I want to benefit somebody. Is that enough for being the cardboard? Maybe, I just want to be sat on. (*Laughter*) Isn't that part in the book about, "Who wants to pity whom?" I want to be pitied—or I want to be sat on—and scrunched down.

PERLS: Say this again.

J.: I want to be sat on and scrunched down.

PERLS: Tell this to the group.

J.: Wow—this is hard to do! (*Slowly turning to group*) I want to be sat on and scrunched down! Hm-m-m-m. (*Yells*) I WANT TO BE SAT ON AND SCRUNCHED DOWN! (*Pounds*)

PERLS: Who are you hitting?

J.: Me.

PERLS: Besides you.

J.: I'm hitting my mother who is turning—who is behind me—and I look around and see her.

PERLS: All right. Now hit her.

J.: Mother, I'm scrunching down on (ouch) you! And *I* am going to take *you* for a ride, instead of you telling me to go, and taking me wherever you want to. (*Yells*) *I'm taking you along for a ride with me!*

PERLS: Did you notice anything in your behavior with your mother?

J.: Just now?

PERLS: I had the impression it was *too much* to be convincing. It was spoken with anger—not with firmness.

J.: I think I'm still a little afraid of her.

PERLS: That's it. You tell her that.

J.: Mom, I'm *still* afraid of you, but I'm going to take you for a ride anyway.

PERLS: OK. Let's put Mama on the sled.

J.: There. You have to sit behind this time. Are you ready? OK?

PERLS: You're taking the lead?

J.: Yeah. I'm—I'm in control.

PERLS: You are in the driver's seat.

J.: I'm not only driving—I'm doing this with, you know, balance.

PERLS: Do you ride a bobsled?

J.: I've never ridden a bobsled, but, I've skied. OK. Here we go. I don't know where we're going at this point. We're just going off.

PERLS: Well, you said that it's a journey into the bowels of the earth.

J.: Yes, but I'm not really sure of that now. I think —I don't really—It doesn't really dawn on me until I realize just how far we keep going.

PERLS: So, start out.

J.: We're going down now. And we're sliding down, and then we come to a turn, and we go around—around—around. I'll see if she's still there. She's still there.

PERLS: Always make it an encounter. This is the most important thing. Change everything into an encounter, instead of gossiping *about*.

J.: Are you still there?

PERLS: What does she answer?

J.: "Yes. I'm still here, but it's kind of scary," she says. Don't worry! I've got it all taken care of! We're having fun. I don't know where this is going, but we're going to find out. "I'm scared," she says. I think I . . . *Don't be scared!* It's just going down and down and down. I wonder what's going to be down here—if it'll just be black. I don't know what she says.

PERLS: What's your left hand doing?

J.: Right this instant?

PERLS: Yes.

J.: Holding my head. I'm—

PERLS: As if?

J.: Not to see?

PERLS: You don't want to see where you are going—not to see the danger.

J.: I'm a little afraid of what will be down there. It could be terrible, or just blackness, or just maybe even oblivion.

PERLS: I would like you to go now into this *blackness*. We haven't come, in this seminar, to talk about *nothingness*—the blankness, the sterile void. But I would like to make a little excursion with you right now. What does it feel like to be in this nothingness?

J.: The only nothingness is that I'm going down, now. I still have a feeling that I'm going down, and so it's kind of exciting and exhilarating because I'm—just because I'm moving, and very much alive. I'm not really afraid. It's more, a kind of terribly exciting and—the anticipation of what I will discover at this end—at the end of this. It's not really black. You see, at the time, it's sort of like I'm going down—somehow there's *some* light. I don't know where from, but just a little.

PERLS: Yeah. I want to make a little bit of a shortcut. Are you aware of what you are avoiding in this dream?

J.: Am I aware of what I am avoiding?

PERLS: Having legs.

J.: Having legs?

PERLS: Yes.

J.: Legs that carry me—

PERLS: Yes. You rely on the support of the cardboard—and you're relying on gravitation to carry you.

J.: Possibly—passively through the time—through life.

PERLS: What's your objection to having legs?

J.: I just—First thing that come to my head is that

—somebody might knock me down. Then I realized that, I guess I was afraid that my mother would—knock me down. She doesn't want me to have legs.

PERLS: Now have another encounter with her about this—that she doesn't want you stand on your own legs, on your own feet.

J.: Why don't you want me to stand on my own legs? She says, "Cause you're helpless, you need me." I don't need you. I can go through life, all by myself. (*Pause*) I can! She must have said, "You can't."

PERLS: Notice the same anger, and lack of firmness—lack of support. You see, the lower carriage is for support, and the upper is for contact. But, without firm support, the contact is wobbly, too.

J.: I shouldn't be angry.

PERLS: I didn't say you shouldn't be angry, but the anger is still—

J.: It's too wobbly.

PERLS: Too wobbly, yes.

J.: I'm afraid to stand on my own two legs and to be angry at her.

PERLS: And to face her really. Stand on your legs, and now encounter your mother and see whether you can talk to her.

J.: I'm still afraid to look at her.

PERLS: Say this to her.

J.: I'm afraid to look at you, Mother.

PERLS: What would you see?

J.: What do I see? I see I *hate* her. I *hate you* for holding me back every time I wanted to even go across the aisle in the damn department store. [*High, mimicking voice*] "Come back here. Don't go on the other side of the aisle!" I can't even walk across the damned aisle. Can't go to Flushing when I want to go on the bus! Can't go to New York, not until I go to college! Damn you! [*Screams*]

PERLS: How old are you when you play this part?

J.: Well. I'm—in the department store, I'm only—anywhere from six to ten or twelve, or, who knows?

PERLS: How old are you, really?

J.: Really? Thirty-one.

PERLS: Thirty-one.

J.: And she's even dead.

PERLS: Can you talk as a thirty-one-year-old, to your mother? Can you be your age?

J.: Mother, I am thirty-one years old. I am *quite* capable of walking on my own two legs.

PERLS: You notice the difference? Much less noise, and much more substance.

J.: I can stand on my own legs. I can do anything I want to do. And I can *know* what I want to do. I *don't need* you. In fact, you're not even here when I *did need* you. So, why do you hang around?

PERLS: Can you say goodbye to her? Can you bury her?

J.: Well, I can now, because I'm at the bottom of the slope, and when I come to the bottom, I stand up. I stand up, and I walk around in this beautiful place.

PERLS: Can you say to your mother, "Goodbye, Mother, rest in peace."

J.: I think I did that in the dream. Bye, Mother . . . Bye. [*Weeps*]

PERLS: Talk, Jean. You're doing great when you talk to your mother.

J.: Bye, Mom. You couldn't help what you did. You didn't know any better. It wasn't your fault that you had three boys first, and then you got me. You wanted another boy, and you didn't want me—and you felt so bad after you found out I was a girl. You just tried to make it up to me—that's all. You didn't have to smother me. I forgive you, Mom. Just rest, mama. . . . I can go now. Sure, I can go—

PERLS: You're still holding your breath, Jean.

J.: (*Pause*) "Are you really sure, Jean?" Mama, let me go—

PERLS: What would she say?

J.: "I *can't* let you go."

PERLS: Now, *you* say this to your mother.

J.: I can't let you go?

PERLS: Keep her—you're holding control.

J.: Mama, I can't let you go. I need you. No. I *don't* need you.

PERLS: But, you still miss her, don't you?

J.: A little. There's somebody there. Well, what if nobody was there? What if it was empty? and dark? It's all empty and dark—it's beautiful. I'll let you go. I'll let you go Mama. [*Softly*] Please go—

I am very glad that we had this last experience, because we can learn such a lot from it. You notice, this was not play-acting, not crying for sympathy, not crying to get control. This showed the ability to explode into *grief*. And this "mourning-labor," as Freud called it, is necessary *to grow up*—to say, good-bye to the image of the child.

This is very essential. Very few people can really see themselves as adults. They always have to have a mother or father image around.

This is one of the few places where Freud went completely astray. Freud thought a person does not mature because he has childhood problems—this is utterly wrong. It is because he doesn't want to take on the responsibility of the adult person. To grow up means to be alone, and to be alone is the prerequisite for maturity and contact. Loneliness is still *longing for* support.

Jean has just made a big step toward growing.

Barry's Dream

B.: I'd like to work on a dream I had, Fritz. In this dream, I'm on some kind of a toboggan run, in a sleigh, and the dream starts where I pick a sleigh to go down this run. It's in the woods, and I deliberately pick a sleigh that's too wide, and the trail is narrow. There are a lot of people around. They see me do this, and I'm aware that I'm doing it. They're watching me. I want them to see I'm picking a more difficult sleigh. So I get in this, and I go up to the top of the run, and I start down. On one side is a precipice and on the other side is a hill.

PERLS: On what side is the precipice?

B.: On the right side.

PERLS: On the right. On the left is the . . . ?

B.: The hill. And I'm doing fine. As I get to the part around the corner—around the turn—sort of at the peak really of the whole run—an animal comes out from the right side, from where the precipice is. It's like a two-headed mountain goat with one head above the other—one head on top. And it comes at me menacingly as I'm going by. I take out my pocket knife, and I jab at it in the mouth, and it stops menacing me. Then I finish the run. And that's the end of the dream.

PERLS: Well, I would like you to continue this. Please continue, what did you do?

B.: I am down at the bottom of the hill. I'm in the sleigh. It's an open clearing, like it's wooded area.

And there are people lined up one or two deep—all just standing there. The sleigh stops. I'm about thirty feet away, and I get out and look toward them. Nobody is moving. Nobody is saying anything. Now, I see myself walking first to the right and then to the left, toward them but in a little zigzagged way.

PERLS: All right. I would like you to repeat the dream. Again use the present tense. And this time be aware of your voice.

B.: I'm going to run a toboggan run in a sleigh made out of bamboo. This is in a wooded area, and I pick a sleigh that's extra wide for the narrow trail, which makes it more dangerous. There are a lot of—

PERLS: Can you hear your voice?

B.: Yes.

PERLS: What does your voice say about the content of the dream?

B.: My voice sounds firmer than my fear. I think I'm more afraid than my voice shows. I also feel my voice is firmer now than it was the first time I told the dream.

PERLS: And can you take your fear along to the dream—to the telling of the dream?

B.: OK. I have to run this race, and it's a toboggan run. It's a dangerous run, and I know it's dangerous because it's a narrow trail and there's a deep precipice on one side. Just one slip and I've had it, and so—

PERLS: Go back once more. To whom are you telling the dream?

B.: I think I'm telling it to everybody here and you.

PERLS: No. I'm thinking you are telling it to your head.

B.: I have to run this toboggan race, and it's a dangerous race because this run is very narrow and there's a deep—

PERLS: Listen to your voice. Just feel again the difference, the discrepancy between the tone of your voice and what you're saying.

B.: I have to run this race, and it's a dangerous race that I have to run, and it scares the hell out of me.

PERLS: Is it really very dangerous?

B.: Yes it is. I'm very frightened about it.

PERLS: And still you're going to do it?

B.: Yes, I'm still going to do it. I don't feel I have any choice.

PERLS: You don't have any choice?

B.: No. All the people are watching. You all are watching me.

PERLS: Oh! So if you don't do it for yourself, you do it for us.

B.: I have to show you—uh—I have to show you something.

PERLS: Who am I that you have to show me something?

B.: [*Long pause*] I don't know who you are. All I know is that I have to show you, and I am afraid. I'm afraid of you and I'm afraid of what I have to do.

PERLS: You get already part of the message of the dream?

B.: I'm not sure I know what you mean.

PERLS: Well, I mean that you have to show that you're not afraid—that you're not a coward. It's from your own very important existential message.

B.: So far that was the most—the most difficult thing I've ever experienced—when you told me to sound like I'm afraid in my voice. That was the hardest thing.

PERLS: Will you follow this up a little more and tell members of the group something you are afraid of and don't want to show.

B.: Yeah. I'm afraid of—uh—Bob. So I sat down next to him yesterday. I'm afraid of Bob, so when we're going to think quiet thoughts I look at him first and say to myself, "I'm afraid you're going to strangle me, but I'd like to be your friend."

PERLS: All right. Could you show me? Come up here. Could you rehearse this with me? How is Bob going to strangle you?

B.: You mean—uh—should I be Bob or—

PERLS: I don't know whether you should be Bob. I would just like to know what your fantasy is—how he strangled you.

B.: You're me and I'm Bob and you say—

PERLS: What do I say?

B.: Uh—I'm afraid that you're going to strangle me and so I start to go like this. [*Moves hands toward Perls's throat.*]

PERLS: Wait a moment. What do you experience?

B.: You're right! That's right! That's what I'm going to do.

PERLS: But one does not strangle people just out of the blue? You must feel something.

B.: Well, that doesn't seem important.

PERLS: It's very important to me, because I'm going to be the victim. I like to know with whom do I have the pleasure.

B.: I don't think I could justify why you should die. This is—uh—this is what comes. This is what I feel. And, of course, now I don't feel it. I'm sort of out of it. I'm just standing here.

PERLS: I don't think you are.

B.: I don't know. My left hand is up.

PERLS: Are you just standing there like the Bob of your fantasies?

B.: No. Not now. I started to.

PERLS: Let's go back. How was Bob in your fantasies?

B.: He stands like this.

PERLS: Go on.

B.: That's all. He just develops more and more power, and then he comes in and he puts his hands on your throat. But I'm not Bob.

PERLS: If you start—

B.: I didn't want you to be afraid of me.

PERLS: If you put your smile on your face, I'm not afraid of you?

B.: It sounds very stupid.

PERLS: Yes. I think it is stupid. Somebody is stupid.

B.: How would I make you not afraid of me?

PERLS: This is rubbish. The Bob of your dream or how you fantasied him is somebody to be afraid of. You try to avoid now the frightening part.

B.: The frightening part would be if I had to strangle you.

PERLS: Yeah, yeah. And you want to avoid this. Now try once more.

B.: I feel both fear and trying to reject Bob. I feel frightened at the same time that I'm trying to become Bob. [*Sighs*] I'm shaking.

PERLS: Can you allow yourself to shake?

B.: It's a pleasure.

PERLS: Could you include your muscles and your shoulders in your shaking? [*Exaggerates trembling*] All right, let's start the job again.

B.: I have to strangle you. Barry, because you said that's what you are afraid of so now I have to do this to you.

PERLS: That's nice strangling. How did you prevent yourself from actually strangling me? What did you feel?

B.: I just felt I had a good grip on you and that's all I needed.

PERLS: Ho! Thank you. Getting a good grip on something, doesn't this frighten you?

B.: That's what I wanted from you anyway—to get a good grip on you.

[*Perls holds Barry. Barry shows much feeling.*]

B.: Thought I needed to cry, but I don't.

PERLS: Oh, yes. You still have a grip on yourself. Let's take somebody else. Tell somebody else what you're frightened of.

B.: [*Long pause*] I'm trying to do two things at once. I'm trying to pick somebody and trying to find out what I'm frightened about.

PERLS: Can you stay with this process? Tell us what you're rehearsing.

B.: I decided to first try to search for something that I'm frightened of.

PERLS: How do you do this?

B.: Well, I start to picture something and just before you said that I—

PERLS: Oh no, you do not just picture something. Picture some *thing?*

B.: I pictured myself out on this point out here by the—

PERLS: Oh, it's yourself you picture.

B.: By the precipice—

PERLS: Yeah.

B.: Where I was yesterday with somebody. She walked out there. I was frightened to go out because there is a narrow place, so I—but I wouldn't stop. I went out there anyway, but I got down on my hands and knees. But I went out there. I was willing to show her I was afraid, but I wasn't willing not to go out there.

PERLS: Do you see the connection to the dream?

B.: Well, I thought of the precipice again, but that's the only connection with the—well, it's just that I have to deny that I'm afraid. I have to show that I'm not. And I wanted to tell about my experience yesterday. I—uh—just met this girl, and she was pretty, and I wanted her to like me. So she says, "Come on, I want to show you this point out here on the precipice." And I said, "I want you to." And right away, I began to get apprehensive because I couldn't see where we were going yet. So we get there, and she—she just walks right out. There's about five or six feet of narrow part and then there's a wide place.

PERLS: Stop this now, and tell us about the girl. Let's start the girl. Write a script between you and the girl. "Come on, let's go out on this ledge."

B.: She says, "Let's go out on this. Come on, I want to show you what this ledge looks like. I want you to see the view from this ledge out here." Me: "Can't we just stay here? I'd like to be friends with you, but I don't want to go out there. I'm scared I might fall off. She: "Oh Jesus! Get lost." Me: "Wait a minute. Wait a minute. I'll go with you. I changed my mind." And she's shaking her head, "Too late, Buster."—One slip. Now, I'm kicking myself. "Chicken. Why don't you just go out there and take a chance." But she's gone.

PERLS: So we get the second message. You have to avoid rejection by a girl. Her esteem is so important to you that you're willing to risk your life.

B.: Well, of course, when I hear that, I—uh—it makes me cringe. It is all so absurd.

PERLS: Cringe so. Cringe and get sick.

B.: "Ah! Well!"

PERLS: Now say that to the girl.

B.: [*Angrily*] God damn you!

PERLS: Get all this into the girl.

B.: You mean that if I don't go out there with you, then you're going to just walk away? You go straight to hell! Get lost! Who needs you! Ahh! [*Disgust*] Sickening! [*Voice very strong*] I'm about half way with this one.

PERLS: It's difficult to undo the projection of rejection. We love our ability to reject people who reject us. We love to project that. We'd rather feel rejected than have the courage to reject. The question is how much poorer would the world be without this girl?

B.: Well, now that's—you know, that's not me talking. That's *you* talking.

PERLS: I would like to have your opinion. I know I'm giving you a leading suggestion. I know that I feel if she doesn't take you as you are, but puts you through such a test, she's hardly worthwhile to be in your world. This is my opinion, but I'm not you.

B.: No. I—uh—I can't take any chances. I can't afford any slips. I can't miss once. It just seems like —uh—a person—a person is—the feeling is—you know, how horrible that would be. But when I say it, I know it doesn't make sense, but that's what I feel in here.

PERLS: Exactly. That's what I wanted to point out. This is one of those catastrophic expectations, and you rehearse, and you live on the basis of this expectation without testing whether the catastrophe will really come about if you tell the girl to go to hell. All right, let's find out what kind of death you would risk. Could you now take it up again and go to your death over this precipice? Go and die. Get over with it.

B.: All right. She's out there. And I'm on the wide part. I'm starting to crawl across the narrow part, and it's real steep on both sides. I'm going slowly, and my one hand misses on this side and—[*Scream*]

PERLS: Now, speak of your present experience. What do you feel?

B.: Relief when I hit the bottom. It wasn't so bad. It wasn't bad at all—only bad falling down.

PERLS: Oh, so the death of a fake hero isn't so bad?

B.: I'm still shaky.

PERLS: Let go. I think the shaking is very important, because when you stood here, you stood like this. [*Imitates*] You had an armor plate on your back.

B.: Well, I don't. I want to hide the shaking. I still want to hide it. I feel that I don't want everybody to see my hands shaking. I don't like the way my voice is shaking—I know it is.

PERLS: Tell this to these people. Pick someone it would be most difficult to confess to.

B.: I don't want you to see that I'm afraid. I don't want you to see that I'm shaking, because then you wouldn't want anything to do with me. You wouldn't think it was worthwhile to bother with me. Or you would just turn away. I didn't want you to see it. I would feel I had lost you. And I've stayed away from you all the time anyway, so how could I lose you?

PERLS: Who's *it?*

B.: My hands feel warm.

PERLS: Who's *it?* Who's *it?*

B.: You. I said you.

PERLS: But say this to *me*. What you said.

B.: What I said to you?

PERLS: Something about your fear of shaking.

B.: I don't want you to see that I'm shaking.

PERLS: Go on.

B.: You're getting me out of the mood. [*Perls stands up and demonstrates shaking.*] You don't shake like I shake.

PERLS: Show me how you shake.

B.: I shake like this, but I mean it. You don't do it as good as I do. Try to shake the back. It doesn't shake fast enough.

PERLS: Tell this to your back.

B.: You don't shake fast enough.

PERLS: What does your back say?

B.: I'm too big to shake that fast.

PERLS: What do you feel?

B.: Well, now all of a sudden I feel some strength in my back. That's the part of me that says you don't need to shake. Just stand up straight and don't shake. Don't act like an ass.

PERLS: What does an ass act like?

B.: He shakes.

PERLS: Huh?

B.: The ass shakes.

PERLS: Could you shake your ass? The fact that you can tell us that you're frightened to shake your ass, is that frightening?

B.: I'm embarrassed to shake my ass in your presence.

PERLS: Could you show us that you're not embarrassed to shake your ass in front of us? [*Laughter*]

B.: For what I'm about to do, I apologize. [*Laughter*]

PERLS: All right. Let's go a step further. When you use the toboggan or slide, you can immobilize your ass, can't you? So there's no need of shaking your ass there.

B.: The danger is falling *off* the precipice. The whole of me, the sled, and everything.

PERLS: But there's no need of shaking your ass. I'm sure that you do not have to shake your ass. You put yourself in that carriage and it immobilizes your backside. I want to go down the same slide, without using the toboggan but to go down yourself and shake your ass.

B.: I picture myself up on top of this hill. The pass sweeps around like that, back down to the bottom—

PERLS: Shoot to the bottom. Go to the bottom.

B.: Shoot to the bottom?

PERLS: Shoot to the bottom. So I would even use this

part of the dream. Start shaking from here until you come down to the bottom. Start shaking at your head or shoulders.

B.: My ass shakes first.

PERLS: OK.

B.: I just picture myself sliding down on my ass with my feet up in the air. And my hands are flying out, and my feet are flying out, and I'm shaking all over. I'm going around this curve and all the way down to the bottom. [*Voice tremulous*]

PERLS: I want you to continue it again and again until you get a spine—thirty-two joints.

B.: Well, now I feel like my whole back is stiffening up. And I—now I sort of see myself again on the top of the hill. I'm in the same position. I'm on my rear end, but I'm sort of arched—in the same position except I'm in control. And I'm sliding down the hill on my butt, and I just go right on down. I'm perfectly fine. I have complete control, and I head right on down to the bottom.

PERLS: Do it again—quicker and quicker and quicker. Go round and round and round.

B.: Can't get a lot of momentum here.

PERLS: Can you feel how you're still holding on to this?

B.: I'm trying to. I'm trying to maintain control as I go down.

PERLS: And you put on control by cramping your muscles?

B.: I am in better control if I'm sliding and I hold.

PERLS: Uh-uh. Absolutely not. You're only in control if you have adequate coordination.

B.: That's so simple that it doesn't fit my—what I think I have to do.

PERLS: How many muscles would it take, really, to give you the coordination to make that turn?

B.: Very little. I could just relax and just slide on down. I've done that a lot—

PERLS: Oh yeah. Good. Come on and talk about it.

B.: I could just relax and slide right on down the hill. I've done this.

PERLS: Come on. Do it.

B.: I'm just sliding.

PERLS: Are you dead?

B.: 'Course not.

PERLS: 'Course not.

B.: Can't get killed that easily.

PERLS: Thank you.

OBS: When did you have that dream?

B.: Just about a week ago. Before I got here.

OBS.: My fantasy when you spoke of the mountain goat was that it was sex.

B.: Ha! My feeling about the mountain goat was that it was important. The only thing that I felt about it was that it—it disappeared so easily. I gave it a few jabs with my pocket knife as I went by and it was gone.

PERLS: I don't want, at this time, to go into the detail of the fantasy content. I think I got the main message that you have to protect your back, your backside, thereby creating bad coordination. You limit your coordination by stifling your trembling because you think shaking is bad. But if you are not free to shake, you are not free to use your physical organism.

chapter 9

LIMITATIONS AND CAUTIONS IN THE GESTALT APPROACH

Irma Lee Shepherd

New approaches and innovations, often welcomed by jaded professionals, may stir up both enthusiasm and skepticism. The skeptic may avoid discovering and utilizing valuable insights and skills; the enthusiast may overextend the usefulness into indiscriminate application, with glowing promises that cannot be fulfilled. It is to the latter that this article is directed. Gestalt therapy offers powerful techniques for intervention into neurotic and self-defeating behaviors, and for mobilizing and redirecting human energy into self-supporting and creative development. The work of Perls, Simkin, and others, as reported in articles and shown in films, tapes, and demonstrations, attests to this. Rarely in the literature of Gestalt therapy, however, is there reference to the limitations and contraindications essential to effective practice.

The most immediate limitation of Gestalt or any other therapy is the skill, training, experience, and judgment of the therapist. Since Gestalt techniques facilitate access to and release of intense affect, a therapist using this approach must neither be afraid nor inept in allowing the patient to follow through and finish the experience of grief, rage, fear, or joy. The capacity to live in the present and to offer solid presence standing by are essential. Without such presence and skill the therapist may leave the patient aborted, unfinished, opened, and vulnerable—out of touch with any base of support, either in himself or available from the therapist. The therapist's capacity for I-thou, here-and-now relationships is a basic requisite and is developed through extensive integration of learning and experience. Probably the most effective application of Gestalt techniques (or any other therapeutic techniques) comes with personal therapeutic experiences gained in professional training workshops and work with competent therapists and supervisors.

Beyond the basic issue of therapist competence, the use of appropriate application of Gestalt techniques hinges on questions of *when, with whom,* and *in what situation.* In general, Gestalt therapy is most effective with overly socialized, restrained, constricted individuals—often described as neurotic, phobic, perfectionistic, ineffective, depressed, etc.—whose functioning is limited or inconsistent, primarily due to their internal restrictions, and whose enjoyment of living is minimal. Most efforts of Gestalt therapy have therefore been directed toward persons with these characteristics.

Work with less organized, more severely disturbed or psychotic individuals is more problematic and requires caution, sensitivity, and patience. Such work should not be undertaken where long-term commitment to the patient is not feasible. The patient needs considerable support from the therapist and beginning faith in his own self-healing process before he can undertake to experience in depth and intensity the overwhelming pain, hurt, rage, and despair underlying most psychotic processes. It is preferable, then, in the initial stages of therapy with a severely disturbed patient to limit therapeutic activity to procedures that strengthen the patient's contact with reality, his confidence in his own organism and the good will and competence of the therapist, rather than involving him in role-playing or reenactment of past experiences of pain or conflict. In short, with the deeper struggles the therapist postpones those techniques that release the most intense affect, although these must be dealt with later in time to reduce major aspects of unfinished business and develop freedom to move on. It is helpful to use techniques to facilitate the patient's reclaiming freedom to use eyes, hands, ears, body; in general, to increase sensory, perceptual, and motor capacities toward self-support and mastery of his environment.

The therapist's willingness to encounter the patient with his honest and immediate responses and his ability to challenge the patient's manipulative use of his symptoms without rejecting him are crucial. It is important for the therapist to listen to the patient's refusal to undertake experiments, at times exploring his catastrophic expectations, at times simply accepting his judgment that he does not have access to sufficient support in himself or from the therapist to risk open confrontation with the terrors within. The challenge to the therapist lies in discerning the fine line between overprotection and genuine acceptance of the patient's final wisdom in the moment. In some instances, the acceptance of the patient's appraisal of the situation is sufficient support for the patient to undertake spontaneously that which he avoided only moments before.

Individuals whose problems center in lack of impulse control—acting out, delinquency, sociopathy, etc.—require a different approach. Obviously, techniques that are useful in freeing expression imply this as a desired goal and may be used by the patient for rationalization of his actions with disregard for consequences and responsibility. Carelessly used, such techniques further arm the patient to continue avoiding the deeper levels of pain that he early learned to avoid through acting rather than experiencing. Here the therapist needs to be able to determine genuine from manipulative expressions of affect, to confront without rejecting, and to support without being exploited. Gestalt exercises in "taking responsibility for" (described in "The Rules and Games of Gestalt Therapy," page 140) are often useful. So is the therapist's willingness to confront patient response or behavior not experienced as genuine with "I don't believe you," or "I don't believe you are finished now," or similar reports of the therapist's own response and perception. At the same time, the therapist needs to be aware of the patient's severely damaged sense of trust and the despair and hopelessness that he wards off by his aggressiveness, manipulativeness, and acting out.

A skillful Gestalt therapist will design experiments to facilitate the patient's working within the therapy session, thus reducing his need to act outside. However, work with acting-out individuals, as with psychotics, cannot be considered without commitment to a longer and often slower process than many Gestalt therapists are willing to undertake.

Because Gestalt techniques, in general, facilitate the discovering, facing, and resolution of the patient's major conflicts in often dramatically short time, the inexperienced therapist-observer or patient may assume that Gestalt therapy offers "instant cure." Even in experienced Gestalt therapists, the temptation to direct or push the patient to a stance of full self-support too fast, too soon, may result in pseudointegration and subsequent disappointment. In many patients, the task of relinquishing their immaturities is a tedious and long-term process filled with tentative risking and retreating, requiring the steadfast presence and support of the therapist. He constantly asks the patient to face his responsibility and at the same time encourages him to take risks in order to find his own support, thus reducing the likelihood of the pathological dependencies potential in any therapeutic endeavor. In an effort to reduce or eliminate transferences, it is easy for the Gestalt therapist to reject the patient along with rejecting his manipulative efforts at avoiding self-support. While the patient is to be encouraged to discover his own values and identity, it is absurd to disclaim the influence of the therapist as model; in many instances, he is a good model of a parenting adult who values the growth and freedom of his "children" (patients or students). Sometimes, however, the therapist's goal of patient self-support may be short-circuited by his own impatience in much the same way that parents restrict their child's development by demanding adult behaviors prematurely.

The use of Gestalt therapy with groups is common, but frequently this amounts to individual therapy in a group setting rather than the usual group approach of extensive interaction and "group process." While there is often a high degree of involvement on the part of the group participants, at times with considerable affect and self-insight as they watch one patient working with the therapist, this approach inevitably reduces time for potentially useful spontaneous group interaction. A skillful therapist may reduce this limitation by directing the individual to confront the group as individuals, to use them for trying out new perceptions or communication skills, or to deal with his projections with them and to get their feedback in return. The degree of individual growth and development in such groups may well compensate for the loss of more traditional group experiences.

A major hazard, however, is the therapist's assuming excessive responsibility for the direction of the group by too much activity, thus fostering patient passivity and defeating his own goal of patient self-support. In this case, the group too responds passively, regarding the therapist as an expert or magician, and themselves as having little to contribute without his special techniques and skill. Certainly this is not inevitable, but can be decreased and modified by therapist judgment and action.

One of Perls's most valuable contributions is his approach to projections as the patient's disowned attributes that he has failed to assimilate in the process of growing up. The technique of "playing" the projections (the disowned roles or characteristics) has proven valuable in helping the patient regain and integrate much lost power, energy, and self-support. However, since any statement that a patient makes about another person can, within this system, be described as a projection, caution should be exerted before denying the reality factors in the perception. When one patient confronts another with his dislike or other strong response, the therapist will have to make a decision as to whether to deal with this in terms of the interaction and relationship between the people —whether to encourage the object of attack to explore his stimulus value—or whether to deal with it as a projection of the attacker. This distinction is especially important in patient evaluations of or confrontations with the therapist. A defensive therapist holds a powerful weapon if he labels all statements about himself as projections and fails to differentiate accurately. If honest encountering is valued, it must be a two-way process. The therapist needs to listen carefully and admit, "What you say is true of me" if it fits, rather than dealing with this as the patient's fantasy, and implying inaccuracy or distortion of perception. The exercise of taking both sides—that is, "This is true of me" or "This is not true"—may provide the most comfortable solution for both therapist and patient. In any case, personal openness and reappraisal is essential.

The theoretical emphasis in Gestalt therapy on awareness, self-support, etc., tends to magnify the role of the individual as individual, master of his own fate, separate and distinct from other people, often with little emphasis on his important ongoing relationships and the effects of the vocational, institutional, and cultural systems of which he is a part. This may mean that relationships may too often be viewed as projections and as clearly secondary in importance to the internal happenings, and the marked influence of family and other external pressures and difficulties may be ignored. The emphasis on the patient himself as being solely in possession of the key to his own destiny and happiness can distort the realities of everyday existence. There is a risk in the temptation to make a valid growing and emerging process into a dictum, a *should,* and thus substitute a new tyranny for the old. Full functioning, integration, and actualization, unless experienced in the moment rather than viewed as end states, can become as cruel an expectation and requirement as salvation. Gestalt therapy's focus on a Zen-like way of knowing and growing presents Western man with a dilemma, both experiencing the value of this process, yet finding little in the environment that supports this way of life. Gestalt therapy may often offer a promise of integration, freedom, and satori that is very difficult to achieve in this culture.

The consequences of successful Gestalt therapy may be that by teaching the patient to be more genuinely in touch with himself, he will experience more dissatisfaction with conventional goals and relationships, with the hypocrisy and pretense of much social interaction, and may experience the pain of seeing the deficiencies and destructiveness of many social and cultural forces and institutions. Simply stated, extensive experience with Gestalt therapy will likely make patients more unfit for or unadjusted to contemporary society. However, at the same time, they may hopefully be more motivated to work toward changing the world into a more compassionate and productive milieu in which human beings can develop, work, and enjoy their full humanness.